Elias Boudinot's

Journey to Boston in 1809

Elias Boudinot's
Journey to Boston in 1809

Edited by Milton Halsey Thomas

PRINCETON NEW JERSEY

PRINCETON UNIVERSITY LIBRARY

1955

PRINTED IN THE UNITED STATES OF AMERICA
BY PRINCETON UNIVERSITY PRESS, AT PRINCETON, NEW JERSEY
COLLOTYPES BY MERIDEN GRAVURE COMPANY

ILLUSTRATIONS

PREFACE

THE winter of 1808-09 had been an unhappy one for Elias Boudinot. Towards the end of October, Hannah Stockton, his wife and devoted companion of forty-six years, was stricken with apoplexy and died within a week. Their marriage had been unusually happy, and this blow might have been more serious to a person not possessing Boudinot's warm religious faith. Samuel Bayard, his wife's nephew, had written to suggest that Boudinot should write his memoirs, and to this he replied in November: "My mind is still unsettled and I cannot set down to business. Your request is very flattering, but even if well executed, which can hardly be expected, you would find it barren & unprofitable, except so far as it would show many instances of the unmerited goodness & Mercy of God."

Boudinot's bereavement, however, was not the only occasion for his malaise. His son-in-law, William Bradford Jr., Attorney General of the United States, had died of a malignant fever in August 1795. The settlement of his estate turned out to be a complicated and bitter affair, and was in the courts as late as 1811. One of the effects was the alienation of Boudinot (executor of an earlier will of Bradford's which was disallowed) and his wife's nephew, Dr. Benjamin Rush (Bradford's physician and a financially interested party). The latter years of both these distinguished men were embittered by the resulting lawsuits and quarrels. The peppery little Rush had a fine time conducting what we would now call a smear-campaign, and he had a ready explanation for Boudinot's journey to Boston. Writing to John Adams 6 September 1809, he said:

Have you never observed a passion for going abroad to attend a guilty conscience? The jolting of a carriage and the company of strangers seem to act as opiates upon it. The gentleman who lately visited you from New Jersey, with the largest house in Burlington and everything in and about it to make it comfortable, cannot stay a week at home. New York, New Ark, Princeton (not Philadelphia often latterly) are the usual places of his resort, but the noise and variety of these places it seems have not been sufficiently soporific for the pain of his mind. Hence his late excursion to Boston. Home is generally the only resting place to a man at 70 who has preserved his innocence in his journey through life.

To this Adams made no reply; in a previous letter to Rush (1 September 1809) he had reported the visit of Boudinot and his daughter to Quincy, and had "found them sociable, friendly and agreeable. The aged Gentleman though afflicted with the Gout and has been confined for some time with it, has lost none of his vivacity or his Memory or his understanding as I could perceive."

But we do not need to concern ourselves further with Boudinot's conscience: our real concern is the journey to Boston, and Boudinot's attractive record of the America of a simpler day and of the friendly and affectionate visits of one of the Founding Fathers to some of the surviving men who had been through the war with him and had been his colleagues in the Continental Congress and in the first Congresses of the new nation. On the twenty-second of June 1809, Boudinot set out from his home in Burlington for an overland tour to Massachusetts, accompanied by his daughter Susan, the widow of William Bradford Jr., and Miss Mary Binney, whose sister had married Bradford's nephew. Nowhere in the manuscript does Boudinot give any clue to the equipage in which the trip was made. George Adams Boyd, Boudinot's latest biographer, speaks of his "yellow chariot with crimson curtains, manned by a coachman and two footmen in lace and powder." Chariots, however, were light vehicles with only a back seat, so we must assume that they rode in a post-chaise, a heavier carriage almost certainly drawn by four horses, one of which the driver often rode. The travelers returned to Burlington safe and sound just one hundred days after their departure, and except for the long and vexing ferry trip across the Hudson, the journey was singularly free of untoward incidents.

In 1809 Boudinot was in the fourth year of his retirement

from a long and busy public career. He was born in Philadelphia, 2 May 1740, a member of one of those Huguenot families, driven out of France by the revocation of the Edict of Nantes, who settled in this country and contributed so importantly to American life. Boudinot was educated in Franklin's Academy and in Princeton, where his father settled as silversmith and postmaster when the boy was about thirteen. Although Boudinot had watched the construction of Nassau Hall and had seen the College of New Jersey established there when he was sixteen, he did not attend the institution. He studied law in the office of Richard Stockton and in 1760 was licensed to practice; the same year he opened an office in Elizabeth Town. Boudinot must have prospered better than most young lawyers, for in 1762 he bought a house and married Hannah Stockton, sister of his preceptor. For the next decade he practised his profession successfully, took a prominent part in the affairs of the Presbyterian Church, and by 1772 was a man of sufficient standing to be elected a life trustee of the College of New Jersey. In politics he was a conservative Whig, but step by step went further into the revolutionary arena, first as a member of the Committee of Correspondence for Essex County, then as a member of the State Assembly and the Provincial Congress. In August 1775 he secretly forwarded several desperately-needed casks of gunpowder to General Washington in Cambridge. Two years later Washington made him commissary-general of prisoners, a job which he carried out devotedly and successfully under the greatest difficulties. In 1778 and from 1781 to the end of 1783 Boudinot was a hard-working member of the Continental Congress, serving on more than thirty committees, usually as chairman. On the fourth of November 1782 Boudinot was elected President of "The United States in Congress assembled"; during his one-year term he signed the treaty of peace with Great Britain and the proclamations for the cessation of hostilities and for discharging the army. The threats of a body of mutinous soldiers forced Congress to leave Philadelphia in June 1783; for the rest of the session the Capital was at Princeton, with Boudinot presiding over the sessions of Congress in Nassau Hall and making his home with his sister at Morven. Boudinot requested the legislature not to reëlect him to Congress, pleading that his "private affairs are become totally deranged"; in early November he returned to Elizabeth Town as a private citizen. During the next few years Boudinot was occupied with Ohio lands, and did not participate in the Constitutional Convention; however, he was elected to the first three Congresses under our present government and served in New York and Philadelphia as an enthusiastic Federalist until 1795. Late in that year President Washington made him director of the United States Mint at Philadelphia, which he reorganized and conducted with great ability until 1805, when he finally retired from public office. Boudinot spent his later years at his mansion at Burlington (still standing but now seedy) with his daughter. He was much occupied with religious studies, published some curious works in that field, and in 1816 became the first president of the American Bible Society. He died at Burlington, 24 October 1821.

Susan Boudinot, the second member of the touring party of 1809, was born at Elizabeth Town in 1764, and was named for a great-aunt, Susanne (Boudinot) Vergereau. As a small girl of nine she created something of an incident at the home of the Tory Governor, William Franklin, where she had been taken to a social gathering. A cup of tea was offered to her. Patriots did not drink tea. Susan took the cup, raised it to her lips, curtsied, then threw the contents out of the window. In 1784 she was married to William Bradford Jr. (Princeton 1772), son of the "patriot printer" of Philadelphia. Bradford had served in the Revolution with the rank of colonel, and had a notable career as attorney general and justice of the Supreme Court of Pennsylvania. President Washington made him the second Attorney General of the United States in 1794 and valued him greatly as a personal friend and lawyer; the Bradfords were intimates in the circle of the Washingtons at Philadelphia which was called the Republican Court. Following her husband's unexpected and untimely death in the summer of 1795, Mrs. Bradford lived with her parents, and she continued to reside in the West Broad Street mansion in Burlington, maintaining it in the elegance and style of Federalist days, until her death in 1854.

Miss Mary Binney, third member of the party, was born 22 September 1786. Although her frail health is frequently mentioned, she survived the trip, married and had three children— one of whom, Horace Binney Sargent (Harvard 1843), was a Civil War general—and lived until 1824. In 1816 Miss Binney became the wife of Lucius Manlius Sargent of Boston, a tall, handsome, exuberant man with a fine Roman face, who belonged to the rebellious Class of 1808 at Harvard. Sargent was one of a score of members of this class who objected violently to the food in commons and left college without their degrees; the rest of his life he was a nonconformist with a comfortable fortune and a fine library who wrote tracts advocating temperance and a long series of articles for the *Transcript* on the old days in Boston which were collected in two volumes with the title *Dealings with the Dead*.

The manuscript of the *Journey to Boston* is now owned by the Princeton University Library. The volume passed out of the family's possession and was acquired by Governor Samuel Whitaker Pennypacker of Pennsylvania. At the sale of his famous library of Americana the book was purchased 25 April 1906, together with a number of other Boudinot items, by Frederick Julian Stimson (Yale 1877) of New York, a descendant of Boudinot's brother Elisha. This Boudinot material was inherited by Mr. Stimson's son, Frederick Burnham Stimson, who placed it on deposit at the library in 1947. Following the gift of the Boudinot collection of family portraits, furniture, china, and silver, by Julia Loomis Thorne, also a descendant of Elisha Boudinot, and her husband, Landon Ketchum Thorne, and the establishment of the Boudinot rooms in the Firestone Library, Mr. Stimson presented the documents to the University in 1954.

The *Journey to Boston* was written by Boudinot as a diary on his trip; the manuscript we now have reveals in several places that it is a fair copy which he made after his return to Burlington. The text is written on the rectos of a blank book, with occasional notes and later additions on the facing pages; the whole Bunker Hill story was added on the versos. Boudinot's notes have been placed with our own, but have been identified in each case. The volume has a half-morocco binding, probably dating from Governor Pennypacker's ownership. The manuscript is written in a remarkably regular hand, and every word has turned out to be legible. Since the present volume is intended to be read principally for information and pleasure rather than to be used for textual study, it was felt that no useful purpose would be served by an exact typographical reproduction of the manuscript. Boudinot's spelling, capitalization, and ampersands have been preserved, but his punctuation has been altered now and then to avoid confusing modern readers: for example, dashes have been replaced by full stops when they were used as such. Some of Boudinot's interminable paragraphs have been broken up. Superior letters have been aligned and abbreviations such as w^{ch}, acc^t, ag^t, have been expanded. One or two evident slips of the pen have been corrected.

The editor has not felt it necessary to burden every footnote with obvious citations of authorities. He has worked with a set of the *Dictionary of American Biography* at hand, as well as the lesser but fuller cyclopedias of U.S. biography. The *Biographical Directory of the American Congress* (1949) has been in constant use, along with William Buell Sprague's *Annals of the American Pulpit* and Franklin Bowditch Dexter's *Yale Biographies and Annals.* Family genealogies have sometimes been extremely useful (e.g., Higginson, Lathrop, Chauncy), sometimes utterly maddening (e.g., Morse, Hubbard). Local histories have been examined for nearly all the towns en route, maps have been studied, and Frederic J. Wood's book, *The Turnpikes of New England,* has been most useful. George Adams Boyd's modern study, *Elias Boudinot: Patriot and Statesman,* has been an ever-present help.

The editorial work on this volume was done in the university libraries of Princeton, Columbia, Harvard, and Yale, and at the New England Historic Genealogical Society. At Princeton, Alexander Wainwright was exceedingly helpful in every stage of the work. At Columbia, Miss Constance Winchell and Adolf Placzek gave much kind assistance. It is a pleasure to acknowledge the generous response to appeals for information made to Ralph W. Thomas of the New Haven Colony Historical Society, T. R. Harlow of the Connecticut Historical Society, C. K. Shipton of the American Antiquarian Society, L. H. Butterfield of the Adams Papers, Clarkson A. Collins III of the Rhode Island Historical Society, Miss Josephine A. Hope of the Brookline Public Library, Miss Elizabeth Eades of Phillips Academy, Carl A. Lohmann of Yale University, Miss Rosalie A. Lang and Robert C. Woodward of the Boston Public Library, Charles E. Baker of the New-York Historical Society, and Abbott Lowell Cummings of the Society for the Preservation of New England Antiquities.

This volume is the fourth in the series of occasional publications sponsored by the Friends of the Princeton Library. Previous volumes in the series are Anthony Trollope's comedy *Did He Steal It?,* with an introduction by Robert H. Taylor; *John Witherspoon Comes to America* by L. H. Butterfield; and *The Rittenhouse Orrery* by Howard C. Rice Jr.

MILTON HALSEY THOMAS

Princeton, 1 November 1955

Journey to Boston in 1809

O N Thursday afternoon the 22d June 1809 I left home [Burlington, New Jersey] in Company with my Daughter and Miss Binney, a young Lady, in a very ill state of health.

Having passed thro' Princeton, Brunswick & Elizabeth Town we reached New Ark, on Saturday Evening and spent the Sabbath there.[1] Heard two excellent sermons from the Revd Mr Richards.[2] This Gentleman has been lately settled here, in the room of Dr Edward D Griffin who was called to the Professorship of pulpit Eloquence in the Theological College at Andover in the State of Massachusets. Mr Richards is a prudent, sensible and able minister of the Gospel. His meek & humble deportment with an excellent gift of preaching with fervency & Judgement, has greatly endeared him to his People.

On MONDAY THE 26TH we sat out for our Journey. The weather has been very sultry, but is moderating—reached Paulus Hook[3] about 9 oClock. This is a most disagreeable &

[1] The Princeton stop was undoubtedly made at Morven, the home of Richard Stockton the Signer (College of New Jersey 1748), whose wife Annis was Boudinot's sister. Boudinot's wife, who had died 28 October 1808, was Hannah Stockton, sister of Richard. At New Ark the travelers would have visited Judge Elisha Boudinot, Elias's younger brother, who had a house facing the Lower Green, now Military Park.

[2] James Richards (Yale 1793) had come to New Ark from the Presbyterian Church of Morristown, New Jersey; in 1823 he became a professor at Auburn Theological Seminary. We will meet Dr. Griffin later in this narrative.

[3] Paulus Hook is now a part of Jersey City. Flatboats, propelled by sail, had plied the ferry route between this place and the foot of Cortlandt Street, Manhattan, from 1764, except during the occupation, not without much

tedious Ferry. After being detained an Hour and a half, we were suffered to go off without the least chance of a tolerable passage. We were driven over to Long Island, and it was not till after being carried almost in every direction, but the right one, by the tide & differing Currents, for three Hours & three quarters, that we reached New York. There is some Consolation even in the distressing Scenes of Life. Disappointments & en-joyments are often so blended together, by the good Provi-dence of God, that comfort may be drawn by the prudent Man, even amidst tryals & difficulties. Tho' our patience was put to the test, yet we greatly enjoyed the varying prospects that continually saluted our Eyes. The Day was delightfull—the weather moderate. The City & its appendages for a while en-tertained us. Then the different Islands in the Bay, with the Fortifications, and the many Ships in the East River, which looked like a Forest, employed our attention & observations. Our Ladies were not deficient in their discreet panegyricks on this unexpected Entertainment. Being driven near the Constitu-tion Frigate, it afforded a new subject of wonder & amusement. It is an elegant Ship, commanded by Commodore Rodgers[4] and was entirely fitted for Sea.

Having arrived so late at New York, instead of stopping as we had intended, to dine, we pushed on our Journey without delay, and after dining at Harlem, where I unexpectedly met with an old acquaintance, in the Tavern keeper, whom I thought

---

vexation and occasional disaster. Robert Fulton's Steam Ferry Boat was intro-duced three years after Boudinot's trip, and put an end to these difficulties. The *New York Evening Post* said 25 July 1812: "The Paulus Hook Ferry has ever been one of the most inconvenient and difficult in the United States. . . . It was a preventative to social intercourse between this city and Phila-delphia."

[4] Commodore John Rodgers (1773-1838) had recently returned from the Barbary Wars and was then in command of the New York flotilla and naval station. The *Constitution* had seen service at Tripoli, but her great fighting days were still ahead.

dead, many Years ago, (William Mariner)[5] we reached New Rochelle in good time. Wm Mariner was a very useful Man during our revolutionary War. He was an Inhabitant of the County of Middlesex in East Jersey. Having signalized himself greatly in the Militia, at the first invasion of the Enemy, he was almost cut in pieces & taken Prisoner. Sometime afterwards, having Exchanged him, he became a most useful & active partizan, and was used by me, while managing the intelligence of the army, to great advantage.

We remained at Mr Pintards[6] to rest ourselves, and particularly Miss Binney, whose great weakness required every indulgence we could afford her. She bears her ride beyond our Expectations. The Roads being turnpiked from Princeton to

[5] In the later years of the Revolution Captain William Marriner and Captain Adam Huyler, both of New Brunswick, were whaleboat privateersmen, operating mainly between Staten Island and Egg Harbor, capturing numerous vessels, terrorizing the local loyalist shipping, and embarrassing the Royal Navy. In a surprise raid on the night of 13-14 June 1778 at Flatbush, Long Island, Marriner captured Major Thomas Moncrief (with whom he had had a score to settle since his days as a prisoner) and Theophylact Bache, New York merchant; David Mathews (Princeton 1754), loyalist mayor of New York, just managed to escape. The British finally sent an armed force to New Brunswick 4 January 1782 to destroy the Huyler-Marriner boats, which was accomplished with the loss of four men killed and several wounded. Captain Marriner had operated a tavern in New Brunswick in these years; around 1784 he moved his business to Harlem. Marriner's Tavern, sometimes called the Ferry House, for he also operated the ferry to Morrisania, stood on the Harlem River at what is now First Avenue and 126 Street. President Washington took his wife and Mrs. Adams there to dine 10 October 1789. B. F. Thompson, *History of Long Island* (New York, 1918), I, 337f.; W. H. Benedict, *New Brunswick in History* (New Brunswick, 1925), 127f; I. N. P. Stokes, *The Iconography of Manhattan Island* (New York, 1915-1928), III, 979.

[6] Lewis Pintard (1732-1818), New York merchant, was the husband of Susan Stockton of Princeton and brother-in-law of Boudinot, with whom he was associated as commissary of prisoners during the war. John Pintard (Princeton 1776), his orphaned nephew, a founder of the historical societies of Massachusetts and New-York, was brought up in his home, which was in New Rochelle after 1774; the house still stands, connected with the First Presbyterian Church at Marvin Place and Pintard Avenue.

this place, with the Bridges over all the small Rivers in the way, makes it very delightful travelling, excepting as to crossing the North River, whose Boats & general navigation, has become the great distress of all Travellers, not by habit drilled to its inconveniencies.

On WEDNESDAY THE 28TH proceeded on our Journey, after having spent our time very happily with Mr & Mrs Pintard, whose situation is elegant, having a full Command of the East River with its Islands, for many Miles. We greatly enjoyed the profusion of fruit, which Mr P is so famous for.

The Turnpike being continued, we rode very pleasantly thro a Country, that on my last Tour to Boston was rendered dreary & dangerous from its horrid Roads. but we found it quite changed and a great pleasure to travel over them.

At 5 Miles we passed thro' Rye a small Village of a few Houses and an Episcopal and Methodist Church. At 6 Miles farther we passed Byram River and a small Village called the Saw Pits.[7] This River tho small (about 80 feet wide) divides New York & Connecticut. Here is a good Bridge & about 10 or 12 comfortable Houses. At 6 Miles farther we stopped at Horseneck, to view the precipice made famous by Genl Putnam, forcing his way down it on Horseback, when pursued by the british light Horse in the late War, and thus effecting his Escape.[8] It is very high & steep with the ruins of an episcopal Church at the Top. Formerly, & at the time of Putnam's Escape, there were 90 Steps cut in the Hill to get from below to the Church, on an Angle of at least 60 degrees, at that time the

---

[7] Saw Pits, N.Y., now rejoices in the name of Port Chester.

[8] A marauding expedition, commanded by Major General William Tryon, royal governor of New York, left Kingsbridge on the evening of 25 February 1779 and reached Horseneck, now Greenwich, the following morning. Major General Israel Putnam (1718-1790) had come there a few days earlier on military business; he ordered the surprised Continentals, outnumbered ten to one, to retreat, and started off on his horse for Stamford to secure reinforcements. Pursued closely by enemy horsemen, and in a shower of bullets, the fearless Old Put made his escape. Putnam Hill Park, Greenwich, now marks the spot.

road, to go down the Hill, led round on a more easy descent, making a considerable length to get to the Vale below. But on the proposal for making the Turnpike, the Inhabitants, to prevent it taking a Course out of their neighborhood, united together and at the enormous Expence of $15000 have cut thro the Hill and raising the Valley, like a long Bridge, have made a commodious, easy descent, which adds greatly to the beauty of the prospect. Since this, they have built an elegant Presb. Church,[9] with a handsome Steeple on the highest part of the Hill, so that in returning, we saw the whole Church to the foundation, at Six Miles distance. The whole View is extensive & commanding. Here are 8 or 10 good Houses, but no Tavern fit to put up at, but one, a Mile before you reach the Church.

At 3 Miles farther we passed the Bridge over the Mianus River, 20 or 30 yards wide. Here is a large Grist mill & 6 or 7 neat Country Houses. At 4 Miles we arrived at Stamford, a considerable Town, with 2 handsome Churches with Steeples, on a navigable Creek, containing an elegant set of Mills & about 40 or 50 Houses, well built & several very elegant, particularly one lately built by a Mr Davenport.[10] Here we laid by a few hours, on Account of the heat of the day. The Country from New Rochelle (indeed from the neighborhood of New York) is very hilly & formerly was a very bad, stoney road, but by means of the turnpikes, is now smooth & entirely free from Stones. The Hills generally well tilled & every w[h]ere tolerably well improved. The Houses, along the road & in the Villages, are greatly increasing—well built—neatly painted (generally white) & beautifully situated, Many elegant Seats; some

[9] Although the established church in Connecticut down to 1818 was nominally Congregationalist, its actual mode of government, following the Saybrook Platform of 1708, was preëminently Presbyterian. The terms Congregational and Presbyterian were used interchangeably as Boudinot employs them.

[10] John Davenport (Yale 1770), lawyer, deacon, and country squire, had served as a major in the commissary department of the army during the Revolution and was elected to Congress nine times as a Federalist.

in View of the Sound, with very extensive prospects. The Country is also intersected with various small navigable Creeks, which render the Communication with New York & Long Island very useful & convenient. We resumed our Journey in the afternoon and at 2 Miles came to Roton River, where we found a large Mill, in sight, at the Mouth of the River, and a number of Houses, with large Lotts, scattered in the low grounds. About 5 Miles farther, we passed a Church and about 20 or 30 Houses, called Middlesex;[11] and at three Miles farther, we reached Norwalk and put up at *Motts*, a clean, neat Tavern, where we enjoyed ourselves as if we had been at a private House. The whole road thick settled, & the Country wears the appearance of Happiness & Comfort. The road generally hilly & broken, but the roads good.

Norwalk is situated at the head of the River or Creek, & carries on a considerable Trade. Six or Seven Sloops, ply continually between this & New York. They have two handsome Churches with Steeples, one Presbyterian, the other Episcopal. About 300 Houses and 2000 Souls.[12] Many of the Houses are large & handsome. Mr Swan the Presb.[13] & Mr Whitlock the Episcopal Ministers.[14] The number of Houses are not many more than when I was here last, upwards of 40 years ago, but are much more elegant & Commodious; handsomely situated, but scattered over a large piece of Ground. This Evening wrote home.

JUNE 29 THURSDAY. This Morning sett off at 5 oClock. At 3 Miles passed Satucket Bridge of about 200 yards long, where they have a large Mill & about 30 or 40 good Houses with several Storehouses on both sides the Bridge, with a neat

[11] Middlesex parish in Stamford was set off and incorporated in 1820 with the name of Darien.

[12] The Town was burned by the British during the War. (*E.B. note.*)

[13] Roswell Randall Swan (Yale 1802) was minister of the Congregational Church at Norwalk from 1807 until his early death from consumption in 1819.

[14] Henry Whitlock (Williams 1798) was rector of St. Paul's Church at Norwalk from 1802 to 1811.

Church. The Creek is navigable to the Bridge, from the Sound.

At 9 Miles farther we passed thro' the beautiful Town of Fairfield, situate on a fine plain, well cultivated. Here are 2 Churches an Episcopal & Presbyterian or Congregationalist, with a large well built Court House. There appears to be about 100 Houses most of them very handsome. At 5 Miles farther we came to Bridgeport—a large Village at the head of navigation, containing 50 or 60 handsome Houses, with Stores & 2 Churches. We passed the Bridge across the Bay or River about 1200 feet long. It is settled on both sides the Bay like a Village, with remarkably genteel Houses. At one Mile farther, along a line of Houses on each side of the Road, came to another Bridge over a mill pond of about 250 feet long.

At 2 Miles farther, we entered Stratford. This is a beautiful Town, handsomely situated & well built. The road from Fairfield is thro a plain, and as good as can be desired. Here are 2 Churches, Presb. & Episcopal, the Ministers of the 1st the Revd Mr Stebbens,[15] of the 2d the Revd Mr Baldwin.[16] They have also a large Accademy & a School House. We put up at Lovejoys Tavern, which was neat, clean & indeed everything as Comfortable as one could wish.

While our Horses were resting, I called on my old Friend Dr [William] Samuel Johnson.[17] I was distressed to find him stretched on his Bed, pale, emaciated and apparently reduced to a second Childhood. So deaf as to hear with difficulty, and indeed scarcely able to notice any thing that passed. On his

[15] Stephen Williams Stebbins (Yale 1781) was for twenty-nine years minister of the Congregational Church of Stratford, Connecticut.

[16] Ashbel Baldwin (Yale 1776) served as quartermaster at Litchfield during the Revolution. In August 1785 he was ordained at Middletown, Connecticut, by Bishop Seabury at the first Episcopal ordination on this continent. He was rector of Christ Church at Stratford for many years, and at the time of his death in 1846 was the oldest Episcopal clergyman in the United States as well as the oldest graduate of Yale College.

[17] William Samuel Johnson (Yale 1744) was then living in retirement at Stratford after a long and distinguished public career. He had resigned from the presidency of Columbia College nine years before.

Nurse rousing him a little & telling him that a stranger had called to see him, he opened his Eyes, and tho in so low a state, his usual politeness had not forsaken him. He took me by the hand, in the most friendly manner & said with a feeble Voice, he was glad to see me. I asked him, if he knew me. He answered no;—but he thought he ought to know me, yet being reduced so low, he could not recollect me. As soon as he heard my name, the good old Gent'n revived—raised himself on his Elbow, took me by the hand, and with a louder tone of Voice, thanked God, that he was allowed once more to behold my Face—called me his dear Friend—said that he had constantly watched my progress thro' life, and sincerely partook in my welfare & happiness. He rejoyced to see me look so well and called the time he conversed with me, delicious Moments. He informed me that he had lain upwards of 20 days in the Gout, which seemed to be all over him. That he was patiently waiting for his great Change, and hoped, with entire resignation to the Will of Providence; that he was upwards of 80 years of Age & suffered exceedingly—the paroxysm of the Gout,[18] having been very severe. He spoke of our public affairs with very great feeling & said that he rejoyced that peace was likely to take place in our Land. That a kind Providence had never forsaken us, and he hoped, it would continue to the End. He very politely asked after my Daughter Mrs Bradford—said she was dear to him for her own sake, for she was an excellent woman, but particularly for his beloved Friend Mr Bradfords sake, whom he had most tenderly loved. That he was great, in his attainments in the things of this life, but more remarkably so, in the attainments of his Mind, & that our Country had met with a great loss indeed, by his early death. That if he had lived, he would

---

[18] Boudinot was well acquainted with this agonizing malady, and suffered two attacks on his Boston journey. "Regular gout" is centered in the ball of the great toe, where the deposit of urate of soda granules causes excruciating pain, but the disorder, as "irregular gout," may extend to many other parts of the body.

have been of great public use, in a day of difficulty. Fearing to exhaust him, as he continued speaking, I took an affectionate leave of him, commending him to the grace of God and praying that his exit from this transitory scene, might be under the smiles of his gracious Countenance. He loudly & most heartily reciprocated those blessings on my Head, and I left him, expressing his gratitude for the interview. Dr Johnson has been a Man of great Celebrity (as a pub[lic] man) from his early life. He had a liberal Education in Yale College—was early admitted to the Bar, where his superior talents, his Eloquence, his Integrity and uncommon assiduity in business; but particularly his religious Character, which shone conspicuously on every proper Occasion, not only gave him the ascendancy over his fellow practitioners, but soon rendered him an Object of public attention; and tho' a strict Episcopalian, but of the most liberal Sentiments towards other denominations. After serving his Country for some time in the Legislature, he was sent home to England as Agent for the Colony of Connecticut, which difficult Office he executed with so much fidelity, zeal & success, as, on his return, to render him an object of public favour & his reunion to his fellow Citizens, welcomed by all ranks of his fellow Citizens. Soon after his return he was chosen President of the College of New York; which dignified Office had been filled by his worthy Father, the late Dr Johnson, in his life time.[19] Here also he shone conspicuously, till domestic mis-

---

[19] Boudinot has telescoped Johnson's career and omitted the most interesting parts. In 1771 he returned from England where he had represented the colony of Connecticut in the extended litigation of the Mohegan Lands case, and was reëlected to the Governor's Council and made a judge of the Superior Court. In 1774 he was chosen as a delegate to the First Continental Congress but pleaded important professional business and declined to serve. As an Anglican and a conservative he remained in retirement throughout the war, refusing to associate himself with the revolutionary movement and yet retaining public confidence. At the war's end he adjusted himself to the new order and was a member of the Continental Congress from 1784 to 1787, where he became a friend of Boudinot. Johnson was a member of the Constitutional Convention in 1787 and joined with Roger Sherman and Oliver

fortunes & declining Health, obliged him to give in his resignation, and retire to his former Habitation, where he seems now about to finish his long & valuable life, in the midst of his family & Friends. His Picture has a place in the public Hall of Yale College, among its greatest benefactors. It has given me great pleasure to see this American Worthy (whom I rank among my friends of a long standing) in the last Moments of his Valuable life, as from present Appearances, I think he cannot hold out more than two or three days. May my life be that of the Righteous, and my latter End be like his.

In this beautiful Town are about 300 Houses and of the first appearance. A considerable trade is carried on here, as they have from 15 to 20 sail of Topsail Vessels, besides Coasters & Packets to New York. Our Ladies improve much, and bear the fatigue of the Journey, beyond my Expectation. Being greatly refreshed by a good Breakfast & an hour or two's rest, at half past 10 oClock, we pursued on our Journey, and at one mile came to the ferry on Stratford, or as the Indians call it, *Ausotonick* [Housatonic] River. This is about 1200 feet wide & had a Bridge thrown over, but a very few Years since; but the Year before last it was carried away by the Ice. I could not concieve why this happened to so apparently well built Bridge, there being several Bends[20] still standing, while so many Bridges have

---

Ellsworth in proposing the Connecticut Compromise, by which Congress was made bicameral, having one chamber with equal and the other with proportional representation. He also served on the "Committee on Stile" and with Gouverneur Morris gave the Constitution its final literary form. While serving as president of Columbia, Johnson was one of the first two U.S. senators appointed from Connecticut in 1789, but he resigned in 1791 after the Capital was moved from New York.

The Reverend Dr. Samuel Johnson (Yale 1714), an important intellectual figure of Colonial America, was the Anglican missionary at Stratford for most of his career, but served from 1754 to 1763 as the first president of King's College, now Columbia University.

[20] Bents were the supporting members of a bridge resting on the river bottom. They were rectangular, and as in house- or barn-framing, were usually put together elsewhere then set up by holding down the sill and raising the upper portion.

stood, over wider Rivers than this. This difficulty was soon removed on examining the standing Bends. It appeared to me that the Bridge was originally framed 2 feet too low—to remedy the Evil, two logs of about 12 Inches Square each, were pinned down on each Bend, & thus secured to the Frame. These I suppose, being a kind of patch work, have soon given way, and thus exposed the rest, and all gave way together. I was informed, that at the head of the navigation of this River, about 12 Miles from the Mouth, stands the Town of Derby, of about 150 Houses very compact & of considerable Trade, having from 15 to 20 Sail of Topsail Vessels belonging to their port, besides Sloops in the New York Trade.[21] It is also famous for Coll Humphreys' Manufactories of Woolen &c from the Merino Sheep, a great number of which he imported from Spain, and thus was the first person that has laid the foundation of this profitable & useful Manufacture. Coll Humphreys[22] was an early partizan in the revolutionary War, an Aid du Camp to Genl Washington, and since Minister plenipotentiary near the Court of Portugal. He married [Ann Frances] the Daughter of the famous Mr [John] Bulkley an eminent Merchant at Lisbon an amiable & worthy Lady, with whom he received a large fortune.

At 3½ Miles we were obliged to stop at the Globe Tavern to avoid a sudden shower of rain. We were detain[ed] a few

[21] In this River above Derby, there is a very large Water Fall over a steep ledge of Rocks, where the Water of the whole River about 150 yards wide, falls about 60 feet perpendicularly which causes so great a spray, as to produce the Appearance of Rainbows in various places in a clear day, which is very grand & pleasing. This we received by Information. (*E.B. note.*)

[22] David Humphreys (Yale 1771) had a distinguished record in the war and was voted an "elegant sword" by Congress for his services at Yorktown. He was secretary of the Franklin-Adams-Jefferson commission for negotiating treaties of commerce and amity in Europe, resided at various periods in Washington's family, and found time to write much verse and a play (*The Yankey in England*) as one of the Hartford Wits. His experiments in sheep-raising were successful, as was his woollen mill at Humphreysville, now Seymour, Connecticut, and brought him the honor of a fellowship in the Royal Society.

Hours, but not so as to prevent our reaching New Haven about
7 oClock. Having strong recommendations to put up at Butlers
Tavern,[23] we stopped there, but at once were informed, that
we could not be taken in, being quite full. We asked for a
recommendation to some other Tavern, the answer was, that
all were full. We applied for a private lodging, but received
the same answer, as there were three Courts sitting in the Town.
Not at all pleased to be thus put to difficulties for lodging one
night, in so large a Town, I contemplated leaving the Town
& going on our way late as it was. However recollecting that
the Revd Dr Dwight,[24] the President of the College, with
whom I was acquainted, lived in the Town, I asked for directions
to his House—was answered that it was but a Square off. I determined to apply to him for recommendation to a private lodging—and though it was very wet, and I had not walked a quarter
of a Mile for many Months I set off—and was directed from
Square to Square till I walked at least that distance. On inform-
ing the Dr of my distress, he declared to me that he did not
know of a lodging to be had in the Town—That he himself
was quite full. He called out (having Company) a Gent'n to
advise with, who gave me no better Encouragement, except
that if I could do no better, he could let me have one Bed. This
however kind, would not serve my purpose. Having a Letter
for Judge Chauncey,[25] on Enquiry, I found that I returned

[23] The public house of Justus Butler stood on the west side of Church
Street between the present Center and Crown Streets.

[24] Timothy Dwight (Yale 1769) was living in a handsome house (illustrated and described in *Old-Time New England*, XLV, 93-102) facing the
Green on College Street near Elm, now the site of Farnam Hall. A man of
many talents, Dwight had been president of the college since 1795, and in
his informed, able, and straightforward way was not only giving Yale the
best administration it had had up to that time, but also the impetus and
direction for its later growth.

[25] Charles Chauncey, LL.D. (1747-1823), New Haven lawyer and teacher
of law, had been judge of the superior court and was a founder and president
of the first agricultural society in Connecticut. His wife was Abigail Darling.
The Chauncey house was on Church Street facing the Green, between Court

by his door. I accordingly stopped to deliver the Letter, when he told me, that he had been informed of my Journey, he had given positive directions to Mr Butler, that when we came, he was to send us directly to his house. That he had lodgings for us & expected that we would come to his House. It was now dark. I accepted his polite offer, and immediately returned with the Ladies & took the advantage of Judge Chauncey's hospitality. We were received with a cordial welcome, and as if we had been Members of his Family. No one could show more generous politeness. This very amiable family consists of Mr & Mrs Chauncey, a worthy Couple in the decline of Life, but of a fine flow of spirits and delighting to make all happy around them and a Son & two Daughters.

JUNE 30 FRIDAY. President Dwight politely called on us this Morning & welcomed us to New Haven. Went with me to Mr Woolsey's,[26] as I wished to thank him for his polite offer of a Bed the Evening before, tho' I could not accept of it. He lives in a very large Elegant House, pleasantly situated with a very handsome Garden. He is a genteel elegant man and treated me very kindly.

Dined at Judge Chauncey's and was more & more pleased with the acquisition of such social, valuable Friends. In the

---

and Chapel Streets. Evidently Boudinot meant that the family at home consisted of a son (Nathaniel, Yale 1806, then studying law with his father) and two daughters. There were two other sons, lawyers in Philadelphia and friends of Boudinot: Elihu (Yale 1796), sometime editor of *The Gazette of the United States* and early railroad capitalist; and Charles (Yale 1792), who had recently married the daughter of Colonel John Chester of Wethersfield.

[26] William Walton Woolsey (1766-1839) was a wealthy New York hardware merchant who was later president of the Boston & Providence Railroad. In 1808 he had brought his family to New Haven to reside while the sons were getting their education. Their home was at the corner of Chapel and Union Streets. The first Mrs. Woolsey was Elizabeth Dwight, sister of President Dwight and mother of Theodore Dwight Woolsey (Yale 1820), president of Yale from 1846 to 1871. After her death Mr. Woolsey married Sarah Chauncey, daughter of Judge Chauncey. Mary Woolsey, the wife of President Dwight, was a half-sister of W. W. Woolsey.

afternoon, went with Dr Dwight to visit the Gun Manufactory about 5 Miles up the River, established by Mr. Whitney.[27] Was greatly pleased with the appearance of every thing about this Establishment. Mr Whitney appears to be a Man of real genius —has had a liberal Education, and appears to have a very philosophical turn of Mind. He rec'd us with great ease & politeness, and appeared much of the Gentleman. It seems to me, an extraordinary institution. Every thing is done by Machinery (moved by Water), of his own invention. He has an extraordinary head of Water which enables him to finish off 4000 Stand of Arms in the compleatest order per annum. On his becoming a Graduate of Yale College, he was applied to, for the purpose of under taking the tuition of some pupils in Georgia. He went with the Gentleman who applied to him, but on his arrival, some unexpected Circumstances prevented his accepting this new station. While in this State, he observed the difficulties the Inhabitants were under with regard to the cleaning their Cotton. On examining the state of the business, he set himself to work, and soon invented a very simple Machine, which fully answered the most valuable & important purposes. By this Machine one or two Men could clean as much Cotton, as a great number of Negroes could do, in a day. He obtained a Patent, which answered but little purpose to him. The Planters of the Southern States, being astonished at the use of this Machine, universally adopted it, without paying any regard to the Patentee. After a

[27] Eli Whitney was graduated from Yale in 1792 and before the end of that year had made his first model of a cotton gin on the plantation of the widow of General Nathanael Greene in Georgia. After various calamities and discouragements at the South, he returned to Connecticut and in 1798 obtained a contract to manufacture muskets for the U.S. Army. He established an armory on the Mill River at what is now Whitneyville in the town of Hamden, two miles north of New Haven Green, and was not only successful in the production of firearms, but by the principle of division of labor and the use of interchangeable parts laid the foundation for the age of mass-production. Readers may find it interesting to compare Dr. Dwight's account of Whitney in the former's *Travels; in New-England and New-York* (New Haven, 1821), II, 286-290.

Contest of many Years—the States of South & North Carolina & that of Tennessee or Kentuckey made Mr Whitney some recompence for this brilliant Service, but Georgia has continually refused this common Justice. He has left the Southern States with disgust and has settled in his native State.

JULY I SATURDAY. Visited the remarkable burying Ground,[28] lately established near this Town. This is reckoned a considerable Curiosity & calculated to impress proper meditations in the serious mind, much better than the absurd practice, of placing those receptacles of the dead in the middle of a populous Town, without the least inclosure. It consists of 3 or 4 Acres of land. Has a large Walk in the midst, sufficient to turn a Carriage in—the rest is divided into plats sufficient to contain two graves in width, and Walks between the plats, every Walk planted with Trees on each side (Lombardy Poplars). The Plats are formed into Squares or small divisions, each for one family, who have a fee simple in such Square. The large Monuments are all placed in one streight line, and the smaller or rather grave Stones, in another. The whole has a very delightful Effect, greater than can readily be concieved. This is the work of the honorable James Hillhouse Esqr Senator of the United States and a Mr [   ][29] and will be a durable monument of their genius's & public Spirit. In the afternoon we visited the College, and was very kindly & politely recieved by the President & Professors.

Examined the Collection of natural Curiosities. The Chemi-

---

[28] The Grove Street Cemetery was organized by James Hillhouse in 1796 and was the first chartered cemetery in the United States.

[29] Boudinot left a space here, but it does not appear that there was a co-organizer; the original group consisted of thirty-two "Proprietors of the New Burying Ground of New Haven."

Senator Hillhouse (Yale 1773) devoted much of his life to public service: as a militia captain he served with notable bravery and coolness in repelling Tryon's invasion of New Haven in 1779; he was a Federalist Congressman or Senator for twenty years, Commissioner of the School Fund of Connecticut, treasurer of Yale for fifty years, and was responsible for the planting of elm trees throughout New Haven.

cal apartment & apparatus under the Care of Professor Silliman,[30] a very agreeable & gentlemanly man, of very considerable Celebrity in his department, gave us great pleasure. The Mathematical apparatus under the direction of professor Day, was very Entertaining—Mr Day[31] seems to be eminent in this Science.

JULY 2 SUNDAY. This Morning attended the Chapel in the College & heard an excellent Sermon from Dr Dwight. It shew him to be the able & learned Divine, and to have a thorough knowledge of his Subject. Indeed the great abilities with which the Dr fills the Presidents Chair in this Institution has greatly raised his Character thro' out the Union. In the afternoon we were equally entertained & gratified with one of the Dr's Systematic Sermons, calculated for the Students of the College.[32]

New Haven has greatly increased, since my former Visit. It contains about 750 Houses and about 6000 Souls, 3 Presb & 1 Episcopal Churches—a large Market House & a Baptist Church.

The College has been newly built. It is now about 500 feet in front & 4 Stories high.[33] The Library contains 7000 Volumes.

[30] Benjamin Silliman (Yale 1796) was just beginning a long and useful career as professor of chemistry at Yale, as popular lecturer on chemistry and natural history in many parts of the country, and as editor of "Silliman's Journal"—*The American Journal of Science and Arts*—a quarterly established by him in 1818 and now the oldest scientific periodical in the United States.

[31] Of Jeremiah Day (Yale 1795), afterward president of the college from 1817 to 1846, Franklin Bowditch Dexter was able to say: "His intellectual powers were clear and well balanced without being either brilliant or versatile, and his life showed the most consistent example of Christian purity and grace." *Yale Biographies and Annals*, V, 148.

[32] Dwight's System of Theology was read to the students one sermon at a time and took four years to complete, then the Doctor began all over again. These sermons extended Dwight's reputation to both sides of the Atlantic; following his death they were published in five volumes as *Theology; Explained and Defended* (Middletown, Conn., 1818-1819) and reprinted in London and Glasgow.

[33] Yale College then occupied the southern half of the block now known as the Old Campus and was housed in five brick buildings in a row facing

The Hall is hung with the Pictures of King George the 1st of Great Britain—The 1st President of the College, Abraham Pierson—Govr Trumbull Father of the present Governor—Govr Yale, from whom the College is named, Dr Johnson & several others.[34] The Harbour is on a Bay which runs up Northwardly from the Sound four Miles, and at the Entrance is about half a Mile wide. It has about 3 or 4 fathom water in general. The City lies round the head of the Bay, on a large Plain surrounded on the land side by considerable Mountains. The Town is laid out in large Squares, one of which in the Center is left open, and elegantly planted with Trees. The State House a large handsome building stands on it—and the Colleges & Churches are around it. The whole has a beautiful appearance.[35] The Houses in general are well built, and many of them spacious & elegant—the Streets are adorned with rows of large Elm Trees which add to the rural appearance of the

---

College Street: Union Hall (1794), the Chapel (1763), Connecticut Hall (1752), which still survives; the Connecticut Lyceum (1803), and Berkeley Hall (1803). The Chapel provided rooms on the third floor for the philosophical apparatus; the Lyceum, an almost identical building, housed the recitation rooms and library. In the Amos Doolittle engraving (1807) a freshly-planted row of elms is shown along College Street.

[34] With one exception, all the portraits mentioned are still on view at Yale. The university has never had a portrait of its first president (*i.e.*, rector), Abraham Pierson; perhaps Boudinot was thinking of the portrait of the founder and first pastor of New Haven, John Davenport. The portrait of George I "from the studio of Sir Godfrey Kneller" was the gift of Elihu Yale (1649-1721), native of Boston and onetime Governor of Fort Saint George, Madras. The portrait of Jonathan Trumbull Sr. by his artist-son John was given to Yale by another son, Jonathan Jr. Governor Yale's portrait by Enoch Zeeman was presented by Hon. Dudley North, M.P. The portrait of Dr. William Samuel Johnson is a copy by John Lee Fitch of the original by Gilbert Stuart.

[35] New Haven Green in 1809 had three buildings along Temple Street: the State House (1763), a two-storey brick building with a cupola, standing north of the present site of Trinity Church (1815); the meeting-house of the First Ecclesiastical Society (1757) on the site of Center Church (1814), with a large grave yard at the rear; and the meeting-house of the Fair Haven Society (1769) on the site of the United Church (1815). The two old meeting-houses ran north and south with the steeples facing each other.

[17]

Town. They have about 20 Sail of Topsail Vessels & a great number of Coasters & Packetts.

Two Miles West of this Town on a Mountain, is a Cave rendered famous by having given protection to two of King Charles the first's Judges, Generals Whaley & Goff.[36] They lived in Connecticut, at different places about 10 Years, when Whaley died. Another of the Kings Judges John Dixwell Esqr, lived many years in New Haven by the name of John Davis, and lies buried in the burying Ground in the Center Square, where his Grave stone remains, with I. D. Esqr deceased March ye 18 in ye 82^d Year of his Age 1688/9 cut upon it. The College was founded in 1700—its present Charter was given in 1718.[37]

JULY 3 MONDAY. Left our hospitable & worthy Friends & set off for Hartford. At 17 Miles, along a fine Turnpike Road,

[36] Edward Whalley, William Goffe, and John Dixwell were members of the High Court of Justice erected to try Charles I, and all three signed the warrant for his execution, which took place 30 January 1648/9. Whalley and his son-in-law Goffe, London business men, were major generals during the Protectorate and Members of Parliament; they were regarded as outstanding enemies of the crown because of their position and their devotion to Cromwell. After the Restoration warrants were issued for their apprehension, and they fled together to New England. They are known to have lived, secreted by friends, at Boston, New Haven, Milford, and Hadley, where they died in the 1670's. In the spring of 1661 they were concealed for a time in the "Judges' Cave" on the summit of West Rock. John Dixwell came from the landed gentry of Kent and was a Member of Parliament under Cromwell. At the Restoration he was excepted from the Act of Pardon and fled first to Hanau in Germany, then to New Haven, where he lived openly under the name of James Davids, married twice, had a family, and joined the First Church. The three avenues in New Haven which fork at York Street and Broadway are named for the regicides.

[37] The Collegiate School of Connecticut was established in October 1701 by charter from the General Court of the Colony. Classes were taught at Killingworth in the house of the first rector, the Reverend Abraham Pierson (Harvard 1668), until his death in 1707. The school then moved to Saybrook, and in 1716 to New Haven, where the citizens were raising funds for a building. In 1718 Governor Elihu Yale of London made a handsome gift to the institution (£562 12s), and the trustees in gratitude named their new building Yale College.

ELIAS BOUDINOT, LL.D.

SUSAN BOUDINOT BRADFORD

MARY BINNEY

we came to Meridan, where we rested a couple of hours. Here is a large Congregational Church and a small episcopal Church barely covered in, and left to moulder away, for want of finishing. We visited a Manufactory of Pewter Buttons, a Tin Manufactory—Japanning—and a Comb Manufactory—all carried on to a great Extent by a Native, who, tho' very poor & brought up a mere farmer, at 18 Years of Age set them all up on principles of his own;—and tho' now not more than 23 or 24 Years of Age, has thereby amassed a considerable fortune.[38] They informed us that 3 young men made 30 Groce of Buttons a day. We passed a Bridge on our Way this Morning 400 feet long. At 2 Miles farther we passed thro' Berlin a very handsome little Village. Houses well built—a large Congll Church with a high Steeple—a large Accademy of Brick two Stories high and a common School House. At 32 Miles from New Haven, we stopped to dine at Weathersfield. We drank Tea at Coll Chesters, to whom we had a letter of recommendation. This is a very genteel Family—we were received with marked politeness & attention. Coll Chester was quite an invalid.[39] Mrs Chester is a charming Woman—very Lady-like & accomplished in her Manners—about 50 years old, but as polite & graceful as if she had been bred at a Court. In the Evening we arrived at Hartford, where we were immediately called upon by Mr Thomas Chester (Brother of Coll Chester) and Lady & Miss Chester. We had the pleasure of being introduced to them at Judge Chauncey's and spending 2 Days with Mrs Chester. She appears

[38] Samuel Yale began the manufacture of cut nails at Meriden in 1791, and after 1794 made pewter buttons; Boudinot evidently refers to his son Samuel Yale Jr. who subsequently conducted the business.

[39] Colonel John Chester (Yale 1766) had suffered a paralytic attack the previous year. He had a long record of service in the war, commanding Connecticut militiamen at Bunker Hill, Long Island, White Plains, and Trenton, and was later judge of the Hartford County Court and member of the Governor's Council. Mrs. Chester was Elizabeth, daughter of General Jabez Huntington of Norwich; she was fifty-three. Thomas Chester (Yale 1780) was clerk of the county courts at Hartford; his wife was Esther Margaret Bull, and at the time of Boudinot's visit was thirty-two.

about 27 or 28 Years of Age, and really is one of the finest Women we have met with on our Journey.

Hartford is situate at the head of Navigation on the Connecticut River, the West side, and alternately with New Haven is the seat of the Legislature of the State.[40] It lies about 50 Miles up the River from the Sound, and is divided by the River, over which was a Bridge, Connecting it with East Hartford. This has been carried away, but is now rebuilding. It has about 500 Houses chiefly of Brick, and contains between 4 & 5000 Souls. There are in it two Congll Churches, one a very elegant one, indeed with the handsomest Steeple I have seen.[41] One Episcopal and one Baptist Church. The Town is advantageously situated for trade, having a fine back Country to support it. The Trade is carried on, with from 40 to 50 Sea Vessels, besides Coasters.

JULY 4 TUESDAY. We passed the Connecticut River about 7 oClock in the Morning in a very convenient Scow, and proceeded on, with a determination to leave the turnpike Road and dine at Lebanon, that I might call on my old Friend Govr Trumbul, whom I had not seen for several Years. East Hartford is a continued Village for 2 or 3 Miles, beautifully ornamented with double Rows of fine Elms. At about 9 Miles we passed a pretty Stream of Water, called Accanong [Hockanum] over which is a good Bridge. About a Mile farther we came to Bolton a Village with a Church & School House. We designed to have bated at Andover 17 Miles from Hartford and to have gone thro' Columbia, both on the Turnpike road, but by mistaking the direction at the division of the Roads, we took the wrong

---

[40] The New Haven Colony and the Connecticut Colony were separate governments from their founding until union was effected in January 1664/5. From 1701 until 1873 Connecticut had two capitals, and the General Assembly met for a semi-annual session at each city up to 1818; thereafter annual sessions were held in the alternate capitals.

[41] The First Church of Hartford, dedicated in 1807 and still standing at the corner of Main and Gold Streets, has an elaborate Wren type steeple; it is now called the Center Church.

one, and did not discover our Error till we had rode 5 or 6 Miles. This was at least 5 miles out of our way. We rested our Horses at a very indifferent tavern—Taylors—and was there directed across the Country to regain our road at Columbia. At 5 Miles we went thro' a pretty Village with a Church & School House, called Gowens. A mile from this, we came to a most enchanting Lake, about a mile long and one third as wide.[42] It is a delightful Sheet of Water. We rode round it & passed thro' a small narrow Valley, which greatly resembled the accounts given by the Poets of the wilds of Arcadia. The lofty Hills on each side, covered with the brightest foliage, interspersed to the tops of the Hills with Laurel in full blossom, repaid us, by its beautiful Scenery, for the loss of our Way, tho' the road was very rough & Hilly. We entered the Turnpike road, a short distance east of Columbia. This was about 6 Miles from Lebanon which we reached at 3 oClock. The greatest part of the road from Hartford appears like a scattered Village.

Lebanon is the least improved of any of the Towns we have passed thro'. There are a few good Houses much scattered, 2 handsome Churches of Brick with a large School House. The lands thro' the Town seem poor & not so well cultivated as in other places. The roads universally good. After we had dined at a miserable Tavern, at the East End of the Town, we waited on Govr Trumbul & Lady,[43] who received us with a hearty Welcome. The Governor is a Man of such soft manners, of so meek & condescending a temper, at the same time of such acknowledged & inflexible integrity, that he is universally beloved by all who know him. As the Chief Magistrate he is the idol of the People, and his usefulness is greatly increased by his uniformly religious Character for many years. His Health seems

[42] There has never been a village in Connecticut by the name of Gowens; Boudinot should have written Coventry. The lake was Wamgumbaug.

[43] The second Governor Jonathan Trumbull (Harvard 1759) and his Lady, Eunice Backus, lived in a house which still stands, not far from the corner of the Windham road, overlooking Lebanon Green.

to be declining, which has given a great alarm to the State in general as well as to his family & numerous friends in particular. He has filled various offices both Military & Civil with great Celebrity. At the beginning of the revolutionary War he was pay master to the northern Army,—resigned in 1778. In 1780 he was appointed Aid to General Washington.[44] He was Member of Congress for several Years and he succeeded Govr Wolcot who had succeeded his Aged Father[45] in the Government, which he has administered to great Satisfaction for several Years.

In the Evening we arrived safe at our friend Mrs. Austins [in Norwich] about 8 oClock, having had very fine Roads & passed thro' a pleasant Country. Our arrival gave great Joy to our friends, and Mrs. Austin & her Mother received us as if we had been their Brother & Sisters. In an half Hour we [were] visited by Mr. Thomas & Daniel Lathrop, Brothers of Mrs. Austin, Mr. Coit & Lady, of the same Family, who welcomed us to Norwich with great friendship & Politeness.[46]

[44] Mr. Trumbul was born in March 1740. He served in the State Legislature for Lebanon several years—and in 1785 was chosen Speaker of the House—and of Congress in 1791. In 1794 he was chosen a Senator in Congress; in 1796 Lieut. Govr. of the State & in 1798 was chosen Governor. (*E.B. note.*)

[45] As deputy governor, Jonathan Trumbull Jr. succeeded Governor Oliver Wolcott the elder (Yale 1747) upon the latter's death in December 1797, and was elected governor annually for the remainder of his life. Wolcott, however, was not the immediate successor of Trumbull's father: Jonathan Trumbull (Harvard 1727), the war governor of Connecticut, served from 1769 to 1783 and was followed in office by Matthew Griswold and Samuel Huntington.

[46] The hostess of our travelers at Norwich was Lydia Lathrop Austin, wife of the Reverend David Austin, formerly of Elizabeth Town, New Jersey. Mrs. Austin was the daughter of Dr. Joshua Lathrop (Yale 1743), who had amassed a fortune in the drug business in Norwich, and his second wife Mercy Eels; her brothers Thomas and Daniel were continuing the family business. Thomas Lathrop had married Hannah Bill. Daniel Lathrop (Yale 1787) was the husband of Elizabeth Tracy Turner and spent much time abroad making foreign purchases of drugs. Their cousin Daniel Lathrop Coit, husband of Elizabeth Bill, had retired from the family firm.

David Austin (Yale 1779) became pastor of the Presbyterian Church of

JULY 5 WEDNESDAY. We were called upon this Morning by Mrs T. Lathrop & Mrs Coit. Mr Thomas Lathrop brought his Carriage & Chaise, and took us round this extensive Town. There are about 500 Houses scattered over a narrow Vale of two Miles. We then proceeded, to what is called the Landing, being the Harbour about 14 Miles from the Sound, up the river Thames, which here looses its name, and divides into two branches the Easternmost is called Shetucket and the West, is called Little River. This River about a Mile from its Mouth has a remarkable & very Romantic Cataract. Thither we went & were much surprized at this surprizing work of Nature. It is romantic indeed, and a great natural Curiosity. A rock 10 or 12 feet in perpendicular height extends across the Channel. Over this the River rushes in a perpetual torrent, with a violence that terrifies the Spectator, on the broken rocks below. Here the passage for the Water becomes very narrow, between two ledges of broken Rocks, one side being much higher than the other. You find among these very craggy Rocks, many of them ex-cavated in a very extraordinary manner, by the violence of the Water, agitating round Stones, that happen to fall on hollows that stay their passage down the fall. Some of these Cavities are

---

Elizabeth Town in 1788. Always an eccentric man, his mind became un-hinged a few years later and he devoted himself with complete absorption to the doctrine of the Second Advent. He predicted the coming of Christ on the fourth Sabbath in May 1796, and attracted a substantial following; their disappointment did nothing to dissipate his delusion, and his continued cru-sading resulted in his removal from the Elizabeth Town pastorate in 1797. Austin then returned to New Haven where he spent his patrimony erecting several large houses and a wharf on Water Street for the Jews of America whom he invited to assemble and embark for the Holy Land to await the coming of the Messiah. This enterprise landed him in the debtor's prison. His wife had meanwhile returned to her father's home in Norwich. The death of Dr. Lathrop in 1807 provided her with abundant means, and she took her husband back and nursed him out of his delusion; he was able to take a small parish in Bozrah, near Norwich, in 1815, continuing there until his death. The absence of any mention of Austin by our diarist makes it almost certain that he was not in Norwich during the Boudinot visit.

[23]

4 or 5 feet deep & of a circular form. The picturesque appearance of the surrounding Hills—the beautiful Sheet of Water above the Falls—the tremendous roaring of the stream down the awful precipice, and the apparent existence of an Earthquake in the beginning of time, as the Cause of such dreadful confusion of huge & Massy Rocks, fill the Spectator at once with awe & delight. Below these falls are some of the finest Mills in the State. We took notice of an Oil Mill[47]—a Paper Mill—a fulling Mill a Grist Mill, a Saw Mill, and those Grist Mills called Lathrops Mills lower down, are said to be equal to any in the United States. Across the Mouth of the River we passed over a large Bridge.

The Port is a good one, at the head of navigation, and there belongs to it, about 20 Sail of Vessels besides Coasters & Packetts. The Inhabitants are very industrious, and carry on considerable Manufactures, of Oil, Paper, Buttons, Stone & earthen Ware, Timber, Watches, Clocks, Chocolate and all kinds of Iron Work. It appears to me that they will not be behind hand in the manufacturing of Cotton goods of all kinds, in a few Years. There is a fine back Country that supports every kind of trade. The Town is situated on a Tongue of Land between the two Rivers before mentioned. The Gardens are principally on the sides of the Hills, and are formed as hanging Gardens (except below on the level ground) and every spot seems to be improved in the best manner. The Meadows along the Brook that runs thro' the Town appear in good state of Cultivation. They are now cutting their Grass, and the Crops are large & good. We found a very level tract, of considerable Extent between the Town & the landing, called the Plains. This has been wholly left with little or no Improvement, on account of its want of Water, none being to be obtained, but by digging 50 feet deep, till very lately, when Hydrants have been established & Water brought

---

[47] An oil mill, in those innocent days half a century before the discovery of petroleum, employed machinery to crush or press seeds, fruits, nuts, etc., to extract their oils.

from a distance in pipes. A number of Handsome, and indeed elegant Houses have been lately built by the Merchants, and it now promises fair to form the handsomest & most Commodious part of the Town.

This City appears to enjoy a very healthy Situation. The fever & Ague is not known here and the longevity of the Inhabitants is full Evidence of the Salubrity of the Climate. I happened, by accident, to see a genealogical Statement of the Family in which I now am, and made the following Extract from it, of the Ages of 18 Children of three Sons, & old Dr Lathrop, the founder of the Family, at the time of their Deaths. [48]

JULY 6 THURSDAY. Miss Binney is so unwell as to keep her room this day. Dined with Mr. Thomas Lathrop in Company with Mr Coit & Lady. This is a most agreeable & friendly Family—two lively beautiful daughters added to our social Circle.[49] Mr & Mrs Coit are sensible entertaining Companions. Mr Thomas Lathrop appears to be one of the most hospitable, benevolent, affectionate Men, that you can meet with. In Con-

[48] Dr. Daniel Lathrop [Yale 1733] died in 1782 aged 70; [his wife] Jerusha Lathrop [died aged] 88; Joshua Lathrop [Yale 1743, died aged] 85; Lydia Lathrop (afterwards Coit) [died aged] 80; Benjamin Lord (Grandson) [died aged] 91. Samuel Lathrop had 4 Sons & 1 Daughter: Thomas Lathrop [died] 1774 [aged] 93, Simon Lathrop [died 1774 aged] 86, Nathaniel Lathrop [died 1774 aged] 80, Samuel Lathrop [died 1774 aged] 65, Lydia [died aged] 64. Israel Lathrop had 6 Sons & 2 Daughters: William Lathrop [died aged] 90, Jabez Lathrop [died] 1796 [aged] 90, Israel Lathrop [died aged] 88, Benjamin Lathrop [died aged] 86, John Lathrop [died aged] 65, Samuel Lathrop [died aged] 61, Rebecca [died aged] 80, Martha [died aged] 80, Benjamin a grandson [died] 1794 [aged] 85. (*E.B. text.*) This list does not agree in all particulars with the genealogical records as given in Elijah Baldwin Huntington, *Lathrop Family Memoir* (1884).

[49] The two lively beautiful daughters were Jerusha Lathrop, 20, who married Pelatiah Perit (Yale 1802), shipping merchant and sometime president of the New York Chamber of Commerce; and Lydia Austin Lathrop, 18, who married Aaron Porter Cleveland, Boston importer and great-uncle of Grover Cleveland.

versation after dinner Mr Coit informed me of a curious Experiment made by an old Seaman, who taught navigation, of holding a small bar of Iron, by the Top to the compass, and it will attract the Needle to the North point—then raise the bar, till the lower End comes near the Needle and it will repel the North & attract the South point. This was entirely new to me, and I shall not be content till I see the experiment & find the fact verified.

This Evening a Clergyman by the Name of *Hart*[50] came in & informed of a remarkable revival of Religion, having taken place within a few days at Colchester, a Town about 14 or 15 Miles from hence. It began among the wealthy & higher Classes of the Inhabitants, particularly among the Women. May God of his Mercy grant that it may prevail.

JULY 7 FRIDAY. This Morning, Miss Binney being greatly recovered, we left our affectionate Friends, not without some tears at parting, deeply sensible of their kind hospitality, and reciprocating the best blessings on each other. Mr T. Lathrop & Mrs Austin accompanied us several Miles on our Way. By their advice we took the old road, it not being so mountainous as the turnpike. But yet we found this very hilly. We began to ascend a very steep & lofty Hill as soon as we got out of the Town; and the Hills continued for several Miles. Indeed the whole Country from within a few Miles of Hartford is hilly, but not quite so bad, as the road we are now travelling, but the turnpikes are very smooth & free from stones. The Hills afford the most delightfull prospects over an extensive Country; which is beautifully increased by the lofty Spires to the Steeples, that constantly please the sight. At about 9 or 10 Miles, we crossed the Country & at about 2 or 3 Miles regained the Turn-

[50] Of the several Connecticut clergymen named Hart current at that time, it seems likely that this was Ira Hart (Yale 1797), who had been dismissed from the Middlebury parish of Waterbury after a fierce row in April 1809, but by December was peacefully settled over the First Church of Stonington. Reverend Salmon Cone (Yale 1789) was then minister of Colchester.

pike, and at 15 Miles from Norwich arrived at *Plainfield*, a pretty Village, containing several very genteel Houses. Saw Canterbury about 2 Miles to the left. In this place we found a large well built Church—a very handsome Accademy with a Cupola & Bell and a common School House. At 3 or 4 Miles farther we passed thro' Sterling, where we found the like public Buildings as at plainfield.

Two or three Miles farther, we passed the Connecticut Line & entered the State of Rhode Island. This was immediately discoverable by the state of Agriculture and the poor appearance of the farm Houses, and indeed the general face of the Country. Thro' Connecticut, a Traveller cannot but be pleased with the high state of Cultivation prevailing in every quarter. But no sooner does he pass into Rhode Island, than he is astonished at the Contrast, without being able to account for the fact. On enquiring into this Phoenomenon, we were answered, that in the Country, they have neither Churches nor Schools, and therefore the Inhabitants are not only ignorant, but careless & indolent. At 8 or 9 Miles from Plainfield we came to Coventry (in Rhode Island State). At 12, to Foster, both small indifferent Villages. We did not see either Church or School House. The Lands very stony & poorly cultivated. The Houses very sparce & rather like our back Country. At 15 Miles from Plainfield, we came to our intended Stage at Fisher. We have rode 30 Miles this Morning, and our Carriage being heavy and deeply loaded, we are obliged to be attentive to our Horses, tho' hitherto they have performed beyond our Expectations—therefore we lay by here for a few hours to give them rest, as this days Journey must be 45 Miles. Having enjoyed a comfortable Dinner, we again pursued our Journey, thro a poor Country—the Cattle small—fields miserably cultivated till you get in the neighborhood of Providence, where at 15 Miles from Fisher, we arrived in good time. Within a few miles of the Town the Lands put on a different appearance, tho' there is here room for improvement.

We passed thro' a beautiful Street lined with handsome Houses across a long Bridge over Providence River thro' the Town going to the Tavern, but accidentally met our Friend Mr Thomas P. Ives[51] in the Street, who would not admit of a denial but insisted on our driving to his House, as Mrs Ives had been looking out for us for several days. We accordingly went. We were received with great pleasure, as if we had been the nearest relatives. It is a most agreeable Family—happily situated in a lofty, cool situation with an elegant, inded I may say, superb House, with a beautiful Garden, on one of the highest Spots in the Town, commanding an extensive View of the City, Rivers—Harbour & adjacent Country. Here we were obliged, by the hospitality & kindness of Mr & Mrs Ives, to consent to stay till next Monday. They laid themselves out so greatly to make everything agreeable to us, there was no refusing.

JULY 8 SATURDAY. This Morning Mrs Ives & the Ladies with her Daughter[52] in their Carriage & Mr Ives & myself in a Chaise, visited every part of the Town & environs. The alterations & improvements that appeared on every hand, since my former Visit, really astonished me. I could scarcely believe it

[51] Thomas Poynton Ives (1769-1835) was born at Beverly, Massachusetts. Reverend William Bentley knew Ives's mother as a young widow, and wrote in his *Diary* (IV, 39-40) that "She was amiable in all her sorrows." The boy went to live with an uncle in Boston, and Bentley was his teacher in grammar school. Later he became a clerk in the house of Brown & Benson in Providence, where his rise was rapid. He developed remarkable executive talent and contributed largely to the success of the firm. In 1791 he became a partner and the next year he married Hope Brown, daughter of Nicholas Brown the elder. The firm name was changed to Brown & Ives in 1796, and this name survived until 1951. In 1804 Ives built the magnificent three-storey brick Georgian house at 66 Power Street where the Boudinots were entertained. It has been occupied continuously by the family, and is now the residence of Robert Hale Ives Goddard, a great-grandson. *The Chad Browne Memorial* (Brooklyn, 1888), 51-52.

[52] Charlotte Rhoda Ives (1792-1881) became in 1821 the wife of William Giles Goddard (Brown 1812), editor of the *Rhode Island American* and later professor of moral philosophy, metaphysics, and belles-lettres at Brown.

possible. It was then a small Town of about 500 indifferent
Houses along a steep shelving Hill, giving but bare room for
the two rows of Houses between the rough lofty Hill & the
River. There was then but 50 or 60 Sail of Vessels belonging to the Port. I now found it a large elegant City, the 3d
in point of Trade in the New England States. It has near 1200
Houses & 7000 Inhabitants—about 12000 Ton of Shipping—
Three Banks—4 Insurance Companies—a large Market House
—2 large well built Bridges connecting the City on each side of
the River—7 places of Worship, large & elegant—a large State
House—a Theatre—an elegant College containing at present
90 Students[53]—between 20 & 30 Considerable Cotton Manufactories which go by Water—together with a very large India Trade.

We were waited upon by the Revd Mr Gano, Miss M.
Brown—Govr Boden—Judge Howel—Mr Jackson Member
of Congress, Mr Kane & Judge Barns.[54]

[53] The elegant College was the building erected in 1770-71 for Rhode
Island College. Five years before Boudinot's visit the name of the corporation had been changed to Brown University to commemorate the benefac-
tions of Nicholas Brown of the Class of 1786. In 1822 Mr. Brown gave
the university a second building which was named Hope College for his
sister, Mrs. Ives; thereafter the original building (completely restored in
1940) was called University Hall.

From the beginnings down to 1800 and later the word college was the
usual American designation of buildings for collegiate instruction or residence. At Harvard there was Harvard College, Stoughton College, Goffe's
College, *et al.* At Yale there was Yale College. At the College of the Province
of New York there was King's College. In 1720 Harvard built Massachusetts
Hall, the first academic edifice in America to be called a hall. At Princeton,
Nassau Hall was completed in 1756, but following the erection of East (1833)
and West (1836) Colleges, it was known for years as North College. Albert
Matthews, On the Use of the Words College and Hall in the United States,
Dialect Notes, II (1900), 91-114.

[54] Stephen Gano (1762-1828) had been an army surgeon in the war and
a physician in Tappan, New York. From 1792 he was pastor of the First
Baptist Church in Providence, the first church of that denomination in
America; their fine old meeting-house, erected in 1775 "for the Publick
Worship of Almighty God and also for holding Commencement in" still
stands proudly on the hill below the university.

[29]

JULY 9 SUNDAY. This Morning, we went with our hospitable family to hear Mr Gano—and in the afternoon to hear the Revd Mr Eels, the first a baptist & the last a Presbyterian Minister. The Churches are both elegant & convenient buildings with very handsome Pulpits & Steeples. We heard two instructive, pious & excellent Sermons. The Presbyterian Church has two Steeples & an excellent well toned Organ.[55] This is the

---

Miss M. Brown cannot be readily identified among the many Providence Browns.

Jabez Bowen (Yale 1757) had been a colonel in the Rhode Island militia in the war and had married a cousin of the Browns. For a number of years he was justice of the state supreme court and was several times elected deputy governor of Rhode Island.

David Howell (Princeton 1766) was one of the original faculty at Brown, but resigned his professorship of natural philosophy after a decade to practise law in Providence. He was a member of the Continental Congress in Princeton when Boudinot was president, and was later justice of the Rhode Island supreme court and U.S. district judge for that state.

Richard Jackson Jr., cotton merchant and president of the Washington Insurance Company of Providence, was a Federalist member of Congress from 1808 to 1815.

Oliver Kane was a merchant of New York and Providence who had married the daughter of John Innes Clarke, a Providence merchant of equal standing with the Browns.

David Leonard Barnes (Harvard 1780) was judge of the U.S. district court of Rhode Island and a fellow of the Brown corporation.

[55] The First Congregational Church of Providence then occupied an interesting late Georgian edifice, with two steeples flanking a tall pedimented Tuscan portico, at the corner of Benefit and Benevolent Streets, which was erected in 1795 and destroyed by fire in 1814. This was an improved copy of Charles Bulfinch's Hollis Street Church in Boston. A building strikingly similar to the Providence church, and still standing, was erected for the North Dutch Church in Albany by Philip Hooker in 1797.

Henry Edes (Harvard 1799), trustee and fellow of Brown University, was minister of the First Congregational Church from 1805 to 1832; during the ministry of Dr. Edes the church, without schism or debate, became Unitarian.

Ezra Stiles recorded in his diary 10 July 1770 (*Literary Diary*, I, 57-58): "Last month an Organ of 200 Pipes was set up in the Meetinghouse of the first Congregational Chh. in Providence: and for the first time it was played upon in divine Service last L[or]dsday, as Mr. Rowland [David Sherman Rowland, Yale 1743] the pastor, tells me. This is the first organ in a dis-

first Instance I have ever met with, of an Organ in a Presbyterian Church. Altho' I have no objection to an Organ in Churches that have been in the habit of using them for a great number of Years, yet I love simplicity in divine worship so much, that I can not approve of this innovation in Churches, that have for time immemorial objected to them. The singing in the Congregation (as in the present Instance) is lost by it, as all is left to the Organ & Bench of Choristers.

JULY 10 MONDAY. With great reluctance, we left our worthy Friends, who had not ceased to pay us every attention in their power, but this we could not do, without promising (contrary to our intention) to stay a few days with them as we returned home. At 2 1/2 Miles, we passed thro Patuckett over a large substantial Bridge across the River of the same name. This is a Village of 50 or 60 Houses—famous for its Falls & Cotton Manufactories. This River divides Rhode Island & Massachusets. At 17 Miles from Providence passed Hobarts Tavern and at 20 stopped & dined at Polleys Tavern—a good House—everything neat & clean. At 10 Miles came to Dedham a handsome, well built Village, with 2 Churches Episcopal & Congll & large Accademy—between 50 & 60 Houses, some elegant, especially the late dwelling of my excellent friend Fisher Aimes Esqr deceased.[56] His Widow & Children now enjoy it. The

---

senting presb. Chh. in America except Jersey College—or Great Britain." There is no reason to doubt the truth of these statements, but Dr. Stiles did not like organs, and he hedged considerably in a later entry, 16 May 1785 (*Op. cit.*, III, 162): "An Organ was erected in Nassau Hall, but there is none there now. A small house Organ was set up about 1768 in Mr. Rowl[an]ds Congl. Meetg in Providence, but it is now gone. These the only ones among the Presbyterians in America."

[56] Fisher Ames (Harvard 1774) had died on the fourth of July 1808, and his canonization by the Federalists had already taken place. He and Boudinot had been in the first three Congresses together and had labored in great harmony. No reader interested in politics should miss the extraordinary record of the long feud between Fisher Ames and his Republican brother Dr. Nathaniel Ames (Harvard 1761) in Charles Warren, *Jacobin and Junto* (Cambridge, 1931).

amiable & inestimable Character of Mr Aimes—His public & private Virtues—His great abilities as a Statesman, especially his mature Judgment & discrimination of Men & Nations, has so greatly endeared him to all Men of Virtue, Integrity & Learning among his fellow Citizens, that his loss is universally regretted, and his Memory honored with respect, Love & veneration in every part of this Country.

The Country from Providence to Dedham is generally poor and in a rough, uncultivated State. This, as thro' Rhode Island is increased in the View of a Stranger, as I am told, in a great measure, by the turnpike Roads having been made to pass by streight lines from place to place, and have therefore gone thro' unsettled parts of the State. Here we left the Boston Turnpike & crossed the Country Ten Miles to Water Town, the Residence of our Friend & Miss Binney's Father, Dr Marshal Spring.[57] We were most joyfully received, having been expected for several Days. Miss Binney bore her ride beyond all Expectation. When we left home, she appeared (and it was the opinion of her Physician) more fit for a Bed chamber, than travelling—And indeed I had no hope of her holding out farther than 2 or 3 days Journey, but thro' the smiles of a kind Providence, she not only held out, but grew better every day, & was the entertaining Companion, thro' out the Journey. Here we rested several days, and leaving Miss Binney with her

[57] Dr. Marshall Spring (Harvard 1762), physician of Watertown, was Mary Binney's stepfather. A Tory by principle, he was nevertheless early on the scene at the Battle of Lexington caring for his wounded and dying neighbors all through the day. Dr. Spring had married Mary, daughter of Henry Woodrow of Philadelphia, and widow of Dr. Barnabas Binney (Rhode Island College 1774), Philadelphia physician, thereby acquiring three stepchildren: Susan, Horace, and Mary Binney. Susan became the wife of John Bradford Wallace (Princeton 1794), lawyer of Philadelphia, and mother of John William Wallace (Pennsylvania 1833), sometime reporter of the U.S. Supreme Court, and Horace Binney Wallace (Princeton 1835), writer of literary, art, and legal criticism, and a novel. Horace Binney (Harvard 1797) was one of the most eminent American lawyers of his day. Henry Bond, *Genealogies of . . . Watertown, Massachusetts* (Boston, 1855), 444-445.

Father & numerous Friends, who rejoyced to see her return to her ancient residence, so much better

JULY 14 FRIDAY. We left Water Town, a large Village, with a handsome Church & School House, and after passing thro' a very thick settled Country, we came, in about 3 Miles, to West Cambridge, being an appendage to Cambridge where Harvard University is; and then thro' West Boston we went over a very elegant bridge about 3800 feet long, including abutments, & which we passed for 1/ toll lawful money, into Boston.[58] It is lighted up at night by 50 or 60 lamps, and has a draw for Vessels to pass. We took our lodgings at a Mrs Hatch's opposite the upper part of the Mall, an excellent House, equal to any private House, and very airy, having a large Garden almost surrounding it.[59]

Soon after we arrived, our Friends Mrs [Adam] Babcock, Mrs. [Nathaniel Cabot] Higginson of Philadelphia[60] & Stephen Higginson Junr[61] of Boston called upon us. Invited to dine

[58] The West Boston, or Cambridge Bridge crossed the Charles from the foot of Cambridge Street, and was opened for travel 23 November 1793. The site is now occupied by the Longfellow Bridge, over which the subway runs to Harvard Square.

[59] The boarding-house of Susannah Hatch, an aristocratic establishment, stood on an acre of ground at the northerly corner of Tremont and Winter Streets. The house had been at one time the town residence of the governor, Sir Francis Bernard, and Lord Percy lived there during the British occupation. The Mall, two parallel walks under three rows of elms, ran along the Tremont Street side of the Common from Park Street to Frog Lane, now a part of Boylston Street.

[60] Nathaniel Cabot Higginson, son of Stephen Sr., was admitted to the Pennsylvania bar in 1790 and two years later he married Sarah Rhea of Philadelphia. In 1794 he died at Dominica at the age of twenty-six. Mrs. Higginson remained his widow until 1815, when she married Thomas Astley of Philadelphia.

[61] Stephen Higginson Jr. (1770-1834) was at this time a successful and philanthropic Boston merchant residing in the large and handsome Bulfinch house at 87 Mount Vernon Street and exercising lavish hospitality. A few years later some risky shipping ventures wiped out his fortune and he became Steward of Harvard University. His wife was Louisa Storrow, and their tenth child was Colonel Thomas Wentworth Higginson (Harvard 1841).

tomorrow with Mr Babcock, at his Seat in Brooklyne—also with Mr Higginson Junr on Monday.

JULY 15 SATURDAY. This Morning Mr S. Higginson Junr called on us with his Carriage & gave us a view of the great part of the Town. I was really astonished at the appearance of Wealth magnificence & taste, thro' out the Town. Every dwelling House, Store & out House have an appearance of neatness or elegance, except in the old Streets, where many of the original buildings yet remain. The trading part of the Town, discovers the appearance of immense business and great wealth. The new Town House[62] is situate on Beacon Hill directly opposite our lodgings on the other side of the Common. It is a superb building and stands very High. I ventured up to the 1st Balcony, and tho' I risqued a fit of the Gout by it, yet I was very much gratified by one of the most grand, picturesque & extensive Views that I have yet seen. Mrs Bradford went up to the small Cupola, which I can judge from appearances, must be 250 feet above the level of the Water. The whole of Beacon Hill, formerly so high, rough, broken & barren, as to render it improbable that it could ever serve for building Lotts, is now almost covered with grand & lofty dwelling Houses, and several Streets well built, wherein some of the first People in the Town reside.[63]

[62] The Massachusetts State House was first occupied in 1798. Boudinot saw this fine building just as it left the hands of its designer, Charles Bulfinch, and long before the architectural mayhem of later years was perpetrated upon it.

[63] Beacon Hill, or Trimountain, in its original state was a considerable eminence with three small hills on top: Sentry Hill (afterwards Beacon Hill), Mount Vernon, and Cotton Hill, named for Parson John Cotton. When the first settlers came to Boston in 1630 they found a gentleman already in residence. Appropriately, he was an M.A. of Cambridge University and was comfortably established with his library in a house at the foot of Mount Vernon near the present Louisburg Square, where there was an excellent spring. The Reverend William Blaxton invited the settlers to live there and transferred or sold to them all but six acres of the peninsula. Prior to the Revolution Beacon Hill was mainly pasture land, except for a few country seats, but be-

J. S. Glennie, "SKETCH OF BOSTON FROM BUNKERS HILL, 7th Octo^r 1811"

Henry Sargent, Hon.Memb.N.A., THE TEA PARTY

Mr & Mrs Higginson Senr called on us—also Mr George Cabbot President of the Branch Bank & Daughter (his Lady being sick).[64]

Went to Brooklyne at about 6 Miles, and dined with Mr Babcock.[65] The Company, the Revd Mr Gardner,[66] the Episcopal Minister of trinity Church in Boston, and Lady—the Revd Mr. Pierce[67] Congregll minister at Brooklyne, Mr Higginson

---

ginning in the 1790s the three hills were gradually leveled off and there was building activity for half a century. Allen Chamberlain, *Beacon Hill* (Boston, 1925).

[64] Stephen Higginson Sr. was a brother-in-law and cousin of Senator Cabot. The Boudinots visited the Higginsons at their place in Brookline 21 July.

George Cabot left Harvard to go to sea, was master of a ship before reaching twenty-one, and made several successful voyages. Thereafter he was active in Federalist politics. From 1791 to 1796 he represented Massachusetts in the U.S. Senate, but he declined President Adams's offer to be the first Secretary of the Navy. Cabot presided over the Hartford Convention of 1814. His Lady was Elizabeth Higginson. The daughter Boudinot mentions was Elizabeth, who became the wife of President John Thornton Kirkland in 1827.

[65] Captain Adam Babcock (1740-1817) was a retired merchant and ship-owner who had lived in New Haven and Calcutta, had fitted out privateers, and had been an ardent patriot in the Revolution. He was the son of Dr. Joshua Babcock of Westerly, Rhode Island (Yale 1724), sometime chief justice of the supreme court of that colony, and brother of Henry Babcock (Yale 1752), erratic colonel of Rhode Island militia, and of Luke Babcock (Yale 1755), Anglican missionary at Yonkers, who was jailed as a loyalist. Mrs. Adam Babcock was Martha Hubbard of Boston. The home of the Babcocks was the dwelling house now designated as 215 Warren Street, Brookline, built about 1742 by Nehemiah Davis and greatly enlarged half a century later when Senator Cabot was the owner. Mr. Babcock had purchased the house from Stephen Higginson Jr. in 1806. Nina Fletcher Little, *Some Old Brookline Houses* (Brookline, 1949), 71-78.

[66] John Sylvester John Gardiner (1765-1830) had been educated in England by the celebrated Samuel Parr, and was an eminent classical scholar, conducting a school for boys in Boston in addition to his church duties. The Anthology Society was organized at his house, and he was president during most of its existence. Dr. Gardiner's Lady was Mary Howard.

[67] John Pierce (Harvard 1793) was minister of the First Church of Brookline for fifty years. He was a professional alumnus or "old grad" long before the type became general in this country, and he is said to have attended sixty-three commencements at Harvard and to have "set the tune" of St.

& Lady the Elder, Mr Stephen Higginson Jur & Sister,[68] Mrs George Higginson, Mrs Nathll Higginson, Mr Hubbard,[69] Mr F. Babcock & Miss Babcock.[70] We spent a most agreeable Afternoon, amidst a flow of Sentiment & chaste Conversation. Mr Gardner seems to be a Man of Letters, but was rather silent —Mr Pierce discovered himself to be possessed of considerable knowledge, was very conversable, at the same time very modest & diffident—I am told that he is a solid, able preacher. His Conversation was serious & instructive. The whole Company seemed remarkably sociable & pleased with each other.

The Country from Boston to this place, is crowded with very handsome Seats and rich, well cultivated Gardens—The ground being very hilly, affords grand prospects in every direction.

JULY 16 SUNDAY. We went with Mr Higginson to Church, at the New South, where we heard the Revd Mr Buxminster,[71]

Martin's to the hymn sung at fifty-four commencement dinners. He carried around in his head most of the contents of the Harvard Triennial Catalogue. Pierce had a passion for recording facts, setting down the unimportant ones— he timed all prayers, addresses, and sermons he heard—and generally omitting what would interest posterity. His eighteen volumes of Memoirs bequeathed to the Massachusetts Historical Society were found to be largely unpublishable. Dr. Pierce's wife was Lucy Tappan, sister of the abolitionists Arthur and Lewis Tappan.

[68] If Boudinot means an unmarried sister of Stephen Higginson Jr., this was Elizabeth, who became the second wife of Dudley Atkins Tyng (Harvard 1781).

[69] This may have been Henry Hubbard, brother of Mrs. Babcock, who was a prominent shipping merchant in Boston.

[70] Francis Babcock, younger son of Boudinot's hosts, was a recent graduate of Harvard (1806); in September 1809 he married Alice Wyer of Boston. Louisa was the youngest of the Babcock sisters and died unmarried in 1824.

[71] Joseph Stevens Buckminster (Harvard 1800) was the brilliant young minister of the Brattle Street Church and an outstanding figure in American Unitarianism. He had recently spent a year abroad familiarizing himself with British and Continental scholarship, and had returned with a large library of scholarly and critical works new to Bostonians; he is largely credited with the introduction of Biblical scholarship into this country. His sermons dealt with human affairs and religious personalities rather than with doctrinal matters, an innovation at that time. Buckminster died suddenly in an epileptic attack in 1812 at the age of twenty-eight.

who gave us a well written discourse, rather novel & ingenious, than evangelical. His manner is rather unusual in preaching, holding up his Notes as high as his face, but solemn in prayer. Mr B. is certainly a young Man of considerable Genius, but I fear has not yet attained to the Character of a well read divine. There is therefore room for improvement as he advances in life. Took a Sunday dinner with Mr George Cabbot in the family way, and returned with him & family to the same Church in the Afternoon, when we heard Dr Kirkland[72] the Pastor of the Church, of whom we had heard a great Character—But in our expectations we were disappointed—His Sermon was serious, and delivered with a desire to be solemn; but neither his manner or address was impressive—There is an appearance of coldness & want of animation about him, that prevents the effect that might be expected from a Sermon well written & instructive.

Drank Tea at the elder Mr Higginsons, with Coll. [Timothy] Pickering who is on his way home from Congress. Saw Mr H. G. Otis & Lady.

JULY 17 MONDAY. Day rainy & cold. Wind at NE & very uncomfortable. Dined with the younger Mr Higginson in Co. with his Parents, Coll Pickering, Dr Kirkland, Mr Buxminster,

---

[72] John Thornton Kirkland was the son of Samuel Kirkland (Princeton 1765), pioneer missionary to the Indians on the New York frontier, and was born at Herkimer and raised in Stockbridge; the Indians named the boy Agonewiska, or Fair Face. He went to Andover and Harvard for his education and took his degree the year Fenimore Cooper was born (1789). It is surprising that he should have made such a poor impression on Boudinot. Other accounts all emphasize his charm and magnetism. At the New South, says S. E. Morison (*Three Centuries of Harvard*, 195f) "his personality won back the younger generation from 'French infidelity' to the paths of virtue, and his sermons, logical, intelligent, and sugar-coated, led the parish into Unitarianism before they realized whither they were bound." In 1810 he became president of Harvard: "one of the most remarkable presidents that Harvard has ever had, and the best beloved; and until the age of Eliot every successive régime was referred to his as standard."

Mrs N. Higginson, Judge Barns of Providence, Miss Rhea[73] &c Spent a very agreeable afternoon.

JULY 18. Storm continues very bad, so as to confine us at home. Mr Davis & Mr Higginson called & sat with us a little while. In the afternoon I called on Ch. Justice Parsons,[74] & there saw Judges Sewal & Parker.[75] Found the Ch. Justice to answer the Character I had heard of him. Under a careless & rather rough appearance, I found him the Man of superior knowledge, easy Manners, communicative and indeed of a sweet & amiable Temper. He is acknowledged on all hands to be a perfect Master in his profession. The satisfaction he gives to all parties in the administration of public Justice, does him great Credit. There is seldom an appeal from his Judgment. The Bar here consider him as a second Lord Mansfield. The other Judges are not without their Share of Celebrity. Judge Parker stands high in reputation as an able & impartial Judge. Spent the Evening with Mrs G. Higginson, her Husband being gone to Great Brittain. She is an elegant, Lady looking Woman.— Her manners very engaging and her whole demeanor that of a Woman of rank. She is the Daughter of my Friend Mr Adam Babcock. She has a fine family of 5 Children.[76]

[73] Miss Rhea was probably a sister of Mrs. Nathaniel Cabot Higginson (Sarah Rhea) of Philadelphia.

[74] Theophilus Parsons (Harvard 1769), as a young Newburyport lawyer, had been active in the framing of the Massachusetts state constitution of 1780. In 1788 he was a delegate to the state convention which ratified the Federal Constitution, and wrote for the chairman, John Hancock, a resolution recommending several amendments, some of which were adopted in the Bill of Rights in 1791. Parsons moved to Boston in 1800, and was the acknowledged head of his profession when he was made chief justice of the Supreme Judicial Court of Massachusetts in 1806.

[75] Samuel Sewall (Harvard 1776) and Isaac Parker (Harvard 1786) were at this time associate justices of the Supreme Court of Massachusetts. Both men had previously been Federalist Congressmen. Parker had been U.S. marshal for the District of Maine and was later the first Royall Professor of Law at Harvard. Sewall, a great-grandson of the diarist, succeeded Theophilus Parsons as chief justice in 1813, but died the following year; Parker was then appointed to this post and served until his death in 1830.

[76] Mrs. George Higginson was Martha Hubbard Babcock, daughter of

JULY 19 WEDNESDAY. Day stormy & wet—confined at home till 3 oClock—then, attended by Mr Channing the Lawyer,[77] went to dine with the Law Society,[78] in Consequence of a previous Invitation. There were about 40 Gentlemen present. The Ch. Justice Parsons presided—Judges Sewal, Parker, Dawes[79] & Davis[80] (of the district Court of U S) were also part of the Company and the Revd Dr Kirkland & Revd Mr Holley.[81] I spent a most agreeable afternoon. The Ch. Justice seemed the Soul of the Meeting. He is a most facetious lively entertaining Companion—The most ready wit, on all occasions, and yet perfectly correct & pure. I never enjoyed myself, in so large a Company, with such entire satisfaction. The greatest hilarity prevailed, with Innocency & Mirth. Seldom has more brilliant wit, from every guest, with more decency of manners, prevailed

---

Boudinot's hosts. Her husband, the son of Stephen Higginson Sr., died in 1812, and the following year she was married to his brother, James Perkins Higginson. George Jr., one of the five children mentioned, was the father of Major Henry Lee Higginson.

[77] Francis Dana Channing (Harvard 1794) was the son of William Channing (Princeton 1769), attorney general of Rhode Island, and elder brother of William Ellery Channing. His wife was Susan Cleveland Higginson, daughter of Stephen Higginson Sr. Francis Dana Channing died in 1810 on a voyage to Rio de Janeiro.

[78] The Law Society was an informal dinner club of the members of the Suffolk bar. It had no organization, nor did it produce chroniclers like the Saturday Club.

[79] Thomas Dawes (Harvard 1777) had been a judge of the Massachusetts Supreme Court, but at this time was judge of the Municipal Court in Boston.

[80] John Davis (Harvard 1781) began his career as a lawyer in Plymouth. He was the youngest delegate to the Massachusetts ratifying convention in 1788 and outlived all the other delegates. After serving in the legislature he was briefly Comptroller of the U.S. Treasury, and in 1801 became U.S. district judge for Massachusetts. Judge Davis was for many years president of the Massachusetts Historical Society, and edited the 1826 edition of Nathaniel Morton's *New Englands Memoriall*.

[81] Horace Holley (Yale 1803) was then the happy and successful minister of the Hollis Street Church (Unitarian). In 1818 he made the mistake of his life and accepted the presidency of Transylvania University in Lexington, Kentucky, where he was slandered and persecuted by sectarian bigots until he resigned in 1827. The same year he contracted yellow fever and died on shipboard returning from New Orleans to New York.

in a Social Circle. Many Toasts were given off hand, on the spur of the Occasion, and often repeated, yet full of good Sense, much point and appropriate Sentiment. I was complimented by one in favour of the State of New Jersey, as a Sister State, which they hoped, speedily to see in full Communion. I returned the Compliment, by giving one in honor of the Bench & Bar of Massachusets.[82]

Drank Tea with Mrs G. Higginson, where I saw Mrs Gore[83] her Sister, wife of Mr John Gore, Nephew to the Governor. She is a beautiful Woman, with a fine presence and very fascinating Manners—indeed all Mr Babcocks Daughters are remarkably handsome, taking after their Mother in beauty & their Father in personal appearance.

The fine understandings, displayed at dinner, and the elegance & beauty of the Ladies at Tea gave us a high Idea of the cultivated manners of Massachusetts. The Legislature have lately shewn their Opinion of the Judges of the Supreme Court, by raising their Salaries—The Ch. Justice to $3000 & that of puisne Judges to $2500.

JULY 20 THURSDAY. Still Stormy. Waited on Mr Otis Junr.[84] This Gent'n stands high in the Society of Boston. He is an eminent Lawyer, and ranks among the first Statesmen of Mas-

[82] This gathering gives evidence that Emerson was doing Massachusetts somewhat less than justice in his famous devastating remark of 1852 (*Journals*, VIII, 339) that "from 1790 to 1820, there was not a book, a speech, a conversation, or a thought, in the State."

[83] Mary Greene Babcock, daughter of the Adam Babcocks, became the wife of John Gore in 1805. They lived at 5 Park Street. Mr. Gore was a merchant and banker, and died in 1817. Their only daughter, Louisa, married the sculptor Horatio Greenough (Harvard 1825).

[84] Harrison Gray Otis (Harvard 1783) was the son of Boudinot's friend Samuel Allyne Otis and therefore "Mr. Otis the younger" to him. Tireless in Federalist politics, he had served two terms in Congress and was at this time president of the state senate. Otis was one of the Mount Vernon Proprietors who purchased and developed the John Singleton Copley estate on Beacon Hill. He built for himself in succession three mansions in this area, and all three still exist; Boudinot was entertained at the third one, built in 1807, which is now 45 Beacon Street. Mrs. Otis was Sally Foster of Boston.

sachusets. He has been a very active Citizen for 8 or 10 years past—among the first who promoted the great improvements in Boston, particularly on Beacon Hill & India Wharf. It was one while thought that he had totally ruined himself, but in the end, it is said, that he has amassed a Fortune of $500,000, and indeed he lives equal to it. He has a most elegant House directly opposite the Common well furnished & with great taste. It is situated on a beautiful Site with a very extensive View across the Bay or Harbour, highly picturesque & varied. It almost forms an Amphitheatre, studded, alternately, with highly finished Seats, cultivated Fields & lofty Woods in large Clumps, so as to form the grandest Landscape imaginable. The numerous Churches with lofty Spires, and the addition of the finest Water prospect add much to the Variety.[85]

Was called on by Solicitor Genl Davis[86] & Mr John Gore. This last Gent'n is an excellent Character—Modest, diffident & unassuming. He is sensible, intelligent and of most amiable Manners. By his own indefatigable industry, and unspotted Integrity, he has obtained a very handsome fortune. Dined at Home & drank Tea at Mr Otis Junrs, where we were superbly entertained with a very large Company—indeed it was a brilliant Assembly of Ladies & Gent'n, and Mr & Mrs Otis did the honors of the Evening with the highest Taste & good Breeding. The Suite of Rooms were the best I had seen—the furniture rich & splendid without being tawdry.

The Ladies were generally handsome & well dressed—Many of them were beautiful & very agreeable. The entertainment was equal to every other appearance.

[85] Boston was originally an irregular-shaped peninsula joined to the mainland at Roxbury by a narrow neck which Washington Street now follows. The west shoreline was at Charles Street, and in 1809 the Common and the streets surrounding it had an unobstructed view across the Charles River and the salt marshes as far as Brookline and the Blue Hills.

[86] Daniel Davis (1762-1835) had been a prominent lawyer in Portland and U.S. attorney for the district of Maine; at this time he was Solicitor General of Massachusetts.

Here I was introduced to Mr Grey,[87] late of Salem, but now of Boston. He is said to be the richest Man in the New England States, and worth at least two Million of Dollars. He is as plain a Man as one of our decent Farmers. The Conversation was very general & sprightly, with much good sense. The Evening passed away (tho a large Company) without satiety or dulness. No room was found for Cards, or other means to kill time—all was Ease, good humor & chearfulness.

JULY 21 FRIDAY. This Morning gives us hopes of a change of weather—about Noon, the Sun broke out & enlivened every Countenance with his Beams—rec'd Letters from the late President Adams, Mr [John] Langdon of Portsmouth & my Brother. Mr Langdon (the late Governor) invites us in the strongest manner, to pay a Visit to Portsmouth, as Mr Adams does to Quincey. Messrs Cutler & Lee called on us.

Dined at Brooklyne with Mr Higginson the Elder.[88] We had a very delightful ride, as there is a Village the greatest part of

[87] William Gray (1750-1825) began life in humble circumstances, and was an apprentice in Salem and later a clerk in the counting-house of Richard Derby. By the age of twenty-eight he was in business for himself and his ventures were highly profitable; by 1815 he had owned 113 vessels and his fortune was estimated at $3,000,000. Originally a Federalist and at one time a state senator from Essex County, he deserted his party and came out in favor of the Embargo; this brought him so much enmity and social ostracism that in 1809 he moved to Boston. There he gave much time to Republican politics but with little success. His last years were spent as president of the Boston branch of the Bank of the United States. His son Francis Calley Gray was graduated from Harvard in 1809 and in that year went to St. Petersburg as legation secretary with John Quincy Adams.

[88] Stephen Higginson (1743-1828) was one of the great merchants of Boston. As a young Salem sea-captain he was called before a committee of the House of Commons in 1771 and questioned by Edmund Burke on the state of feeling in Massachusetts. He was a delegate to the Continental Congress in 1782-1783 and later Navy agent in Boston. He was a staunch Federalist, but did not neglect his business affairs for politics. In 1798 he purchased land at the corner of Warren and Heath Streets in Brookline and was one of the earliest Bostonians to have a summer residence there; his house is no longer standing.

the way. Here we found Mr Perkins,[89] Mr Otis, Mr Jackson, an old acquaintance[90]—Mr Stoughton & Lady (Spanish Consul)[91] Mr G Cabbot & Lady—Mrs N. Higginson, Mr S. Higginson & Lady & Mr Babcock & Lady. This Villa is very elegant —The grounds around it, laid out much in the English Style —The Shrubbery & Forest Trees extremely well arranged— The Walks beautifully romantic—The Kitchen garden at a distance, & thro' which the Walks wind so as to extend them about a quarter of a mile, all bordered with Grapes & Flowers —The whole enclosed partly by a Hedge of Lombardy Poplars nicely cut, and partly by stone fence, creates a beautiful variety that enchants the Eye.

Miss Binney paid us a Visit this Morning, with Mr Morse & Lady[92] from Water Town. She has gained Strength & Color surprizingly, so that our great fears on her account, thro' the goodness of God, have been removed.

JULY 22 SATURDAY. This Morning, wrote to Dr Wharton[93]

[89] The Mr. Perkins mentioned was undoubtedly Thomas Handasyd, James, or Samuel Gardner Perkins. These brothers were famous Boston merchants and all had homes in Brookline.

[90] Jonathan Jackson (Harvard 1761) had been a delegate at the Continental Congress with Boudinot; he was later U.S. marshal for Massachusetts under President Washington and treasurer of the Commonwealth and of the Harvard corporation.

[91] Don Juan Stoughton was Spanish consul in Boston for over two decades and lived on the north side of Franklin Place, opposite the Tontine Crescent. He was chairman of a committee which raised the funds to build a Catholic church in Boston, and of the $16,153 subscribed, $3433 was given by Protestants, President Adams heading the list. With these funds, Holy Cross Church on Franklin Place was built by Bulfinch; it was dedicated in 1803. Stoughton's wife was Anne Margaret DeNeufville, a widow, to whom he was married at Cambridge in 1799.

[92] Dr. Eliakim Morse (1759-1858) had studied medicine with his father, the Reverend Ebenezer Morse (Harvard 1737), loyalist minister of the North Parish of Shrewsbury, and had practised in Woodstock, Connecticut. He was later engaged in the London trade, and at one time owned the *Galen*, the only packet running between that city and Boston. *New England Historical and Genealogical Register*, XI, 184. His Lady was Mary Hunt of Watertown.

[93] Charles Henry Wharton (1748-1833) was rector of St. Mary's Church

& my Brother. Sent Genll Cummings Letter to his Son, per Post to Andover.[94] Visited the State House again—The Senate Chamber, the Representatives Chamber & Council's room are all large & Commodious—That of the Representatives being found too high for the Members being heard, they have effectually remedied the evil by a kind of large Umbrella suspended from the Cieling, over the Heads of the Members.

Received a Visit from Mrs Adams (the late Presidents Lady) and her Niece Miss [Lydia] Smith. Dined at Mr Babcocks, whose attention & politeness are unwearied. We lost our Way, and kept them waiting till 4 oClock, after travelling hard for 2 hours. Our Company consisted of the Revd Mr Pierce & Lady—Mr & Mrs Cutler—Mr Ingersol[95]—Mrs N. Higginson &c &c

JULY 23 SUNDAY. Confined all day by a slight fit of the Gout. Mr Cabbot spent part of the Evening with me.

JULY 24 MONDAY. After a painful night, the paroxysm of the disorder abated and I began to grow better. Called on by Mr Babcock, Mr Higginson, Judge Davis, Mr Stoughton & Mrs

---

and friend and next-door neighbor of Boudinot in Burlington. He belonged to an old Maryland family, was educated by the Jesuits at Saint-Omer and Liège and ordained a priest, but while serving as chaplain in Worcester, England, he changed his views and renounced Catholicism. He returned to America at the end of the Revolution and became one of the most scholarly and influential clergymen of the Protestant Episcopal church. During part of the year 1801 he was president of Columbia College.

[94] General John Noble Cumming (Princeton 1776) lived on Broad Street in New Ark and was the father of Hooper Cumming, divinity student at Andover; he had been a lieutenant colonel of Jersey militia in the Revolution, and succeeded Boudinot's brother Elisha as president of the Newark Banking & Insurance Company.

[95] Nathaniel Ingersoll (1778-1826), native of Salem and onetime sea-captain, was the husband of the Babcocks' eldest daughter, Eliza. When his father-in-law bought the Davis-Cabot house from Stephen Higginson Jr. in 1806, Ingersoll bought an adjacent part of the estate and erected a large house (now 135 Warren Street) which was later owned by John Lowell Gardner, father-in-law of the fabulous Mrs. Jack Gardner.

Dr Warren, daughter of Mr Mason.[96] The agreeable conversa-
tion of these Gentlemen diverted my Confinement, and pro-
moted a speedy end to my disorder. Mrs Bradford went to
Chelsea about 6 Miles to see Mrs Hill. Dined at Home. Drank
Tea at Mrs J [ames] Perkins Brooklyne—received Letters from
Mr Bayard.[97]

JULY 25 TUESDAY. Received Letters from J. M. Wallace Esq.
& Daughter.[98] Mr Josiah Quincey called & politely invited us
to Quincey.[99] Drank Tea with Mr Isaac P. Davis & Lady (Brother to the Judge)[100] with Mrs Stephen Higginson, Mrs G. Higginson & Mrs N. Higginson. Here we saw a most striking picture of our Friend Mr Fisher Aimes deceased.

JULY 26 WEDNESDAY. Went to Quincy to dine with Mr
Adams,[101] by the road that leads over Milton Hill. The Road

[96] Mrs. Dr. Warren was Susan Powell Mason, daughter of Jonathan Mason
(Princeton 1774), distinguished Boston lawyer and Federalist senator and
congressman; she was the wife of Dr. John Collins Warren (Harvard 1797),
one of the leading surgeons of his day, member of the *Monthly Anthology*
group, a founder of the Boston Athenaeum, and Hersey Professor of Anatomy
and Surgery at Harvard.

[97] Samuel Bayard (Princeton 1784), sometime clerk of the Federal Supreme Court and one of the founders of the New-York Historical Society
was at this time a lawyer and politician in Princeton, residing on what is now
Bayard Lane. His wife was Martha Pintard, Boudinot's niece.

[98] Joshua Maddox Wallace (College of Philadelphia 1767) was the husband of Tace Bradford, whose brother William Bradford married Susan
Boudinot, and whose sister Rachel Bradford was the second wife of Boudinot's brother Elisha of New Ark. The daughter mentioned was probably
Mary Maddox Wallace. John Bradford Wallace, second son of the Wallaces,
married Susan Binney.

[99] Josiah Quincy (Harvard 1790) was at this time a Member of Congress.
Later he served for several years in the state legislature and was for five years
a most energetic and enterprising mayor of Boston. He was president of
Harvard from 1829 to 1845. Boudinot made no record of a visit to the family
seat at Quincy.

[100] Isaac P Davis (1771-1855) and his brother Judge John Davis were
natives of Plymouth. Isaac was a manufacturer of cordage in Boston and keeper
of the cabinet of the Massachusetts Historical Society; his Lady was Susan,
daughter of Dr. David Jackson of Philadelphia.

[101] John Adams (Harvard 1755), the first, and one of the most unhappy

is fine—The Villas on the way are really superb & magnificent; but when we passed the Bridge & gained the Summit of Milton Hill, we were surprised & gratified with a prospect surpassing any thing we had yet seen. A beautifull River, called Neponset, meandering thro' a large, extensive Meadow, with here & there a grand Mound of tall timber Trees—a number of beautiful Islands in the Bay—a distant view of Cape Ann bounding the Bay to the North East—the open Ocean at about 20 Miles distance, but full in view from our high situation—The numerous Churches & Steeples on every side, and a multitude of handsome Country Seats upon the surrounding Hills in every direction but one—a distant light House, with about 20 Vessels under Sail, formed one of the most enchanting prospects, that could engage the human Eye.

We were received by Mr & Mrs Adams & family with great affection, and our visit really seemed to be gratifying to them. At dinner & soon after, a large Company of 12 or 14 Gentlemen & Ladies assembled, having been invited for the purpose of seeing us, & we spent a very sociable day. A Thunder Storm arose and detained us till Sunset, by which we lost the beauties of a different road, we were advised to return by, as affording agreeable Views of the Country. On our return, found Cards from Mr & Mrs Gerry from *Charles Town*.[102]

JULY 27 THURSDAY. Morning so lowering as not fit for walk-

---

residents of the White House, was now back in Quincy, where his years of retirement extended to twenty-five, the same number he had spent in public life. Madison's appointment of John Quincy Adams to be minister to St. Petersburg in 1809 had pleased the old statesman; it seemed almost a recognition of himself. Abigail, his able and intelligent wife, daughter of Parson Smith of Weymouth, died in 1818, half a dozen years too soon to see her son President of the United States.

[102] No appropriate Gerrys can be found in Charlestown in 1809, and this editor suspects a slip of Boudinot's pen. Elbridge Gerry (Harvard 1762) and his wife Ann Thompson were then living at Elmwood (after 1818 the Lowell place) in Cambridge. Gerry had crossed swords more than once with Boudinot in Congress, but this would not have prevented him from paying his respects to the venerable visitor to Boston.

ing. Our family increased—It now consists of Major Ludson & Lady & Daughter—Mr Wood—Judge Tudor, Mr Leonard & Mr Newbold & Wife—Mr Rhodes, Dr Hamilton & Lady, Major Eccleston & a Mr Otis.[103]

Went to Watertown & dined, on Invitation, with Dr Morse a very genteel family, who have treated us with great attention & politeness. Here we saw Major Pinkney & family & Mr Bull & Lady all from South Carolina—Mr Codman & Lady, Mr Coffin &c with Miss Binney. The Situation of Dr Morse's House is on a pretty lofty Hill—It is large & well built with handsome Gardens & out Houses. It commands a delightful View of the whole Village of Watertown and the Hills at a few Miles distance. Lodged at Dr Springs.

JULY 28 FRIDAY. Took an early dinner with Dr Spring and went to Cambridge, to hear the Honble John Quincey Adams deliver his farewell Lecture to his Class in College, as he is to sail next week for Petersburgh in Russia, to which Court he is sent as Minister plenipotentiary from this Country.[104] The Hall was so much crowded when we arrived, that the Ladies could not get in & I was obliged to stand to my great distress. The Lecture was written in an elegant style—very impressive & entertaining; and delivered in a masterly manner. It gave universal satisfaction to a very crowded & attentive Audience. Har-

---

[103] Of the new boarders who turned up at Mrs. Hatch's, only Judge Tudor can be positively identified. Boudinot notes that the Ludsons, Mr. Rhodes, and the Hamiltons were "from Carolina."

William Tudor (Harvard 1769) was attached to Washington's staff as colonel and judge-advocate-general of the army from 1775 to 1778. He was at this time Secretary of State of Massachusetts. Frederic Tudor, who inaugurated the shipping of boatloads of ice from Boston to the tropics, was his son.

[104] John Quincy Adams (Harvard 1787) held the Boylston Professorship of Rhetoric and Oratory from 1806 to 1809, though he was not in residence. He was in the Senate much of that time and delivered his lectures in the intervals of his public duties; they were published in two volumes at Cambridge in 1810 with the title *Lectures on Rhetoric and Oratory delivered to the Classes of Senior and Junior Sophisters in Harvard University.*

vard College, or rather University, in this Town was founded
in the Year 1638 & was named after its greatest individual bene-
factor, the Revd Mr John Harvard of Charles Town, who died
that year & left a Legacy of £779 for the use of the public
School in New Town, now Cambridge, to which School the
general Court had given £400 two years before. It became a
Corporation by Charter in 1650, & took its present Name.[105]
The Trustees, were the Governor, Deputy Governor & Magis-
trates (Council & Senate) for the time being—And the Ministers of the Six next adjacent Towns. It now has five fellows—
a President—Eight Professors & four Tutors. The Village of
Cambridge in which the University is situated, is pleasant &
rural—It is built on a large plain of good Land, and the Houses
are generally very good & handsomely built. There are a number of Gentlemen's Seats around the Town, which make a fine
Appearance. The Town is about 4 Miles westward of Boston.
The Colleges are Harvard Hall—Massachusets Hall—Hollis
Hall and Holden Chapel. The Library is large & well chosen,
consisting of 15000 Volumes, advantageously placed in Alcoves
which are very convenient. There are 5 Alcoves on each side,
with a window in each alcove, and the name of the Donor over
the Entrance in large gold Letters.[106] There are also several
fine Pictures of the Benefactors of the Institution, done in Boston, and equal to the works of the first Artists in Europe. The
Philosophical Apparatus is very compleat & Cost upwards of

[105] On 28 October 1636 the General Court of the Massachusetts Bay
Colony voted 400*l* towards a "schoale or colledge" and Harvard uses this
as its founding date. Harvard's first charter, still in force, was obtained from
the General Court 31 May 1650. The name Harvard College had been given
to the institution by the same body 13 March 1638/9.

[106] Most of the college library had been destroyed in the burning of the
building called Harvard College 24 January 1764. In the new Harvard Hall
of 1766, still standing but much altered, the library was installed in the upper
west chamber, as Boudinot describes it, with the names of the benefactors
"emblazoned in blue and gold, as in Duke Humphrey's Library at the Bodleian." S. E. Morison, *Three Centuries of Harvard* (Cambridge, 1936), 96-
97.

£2000 lawful Money—a very elegant Orrery made by a native of Massachusetts—After forming his plan, he heard of the famous Orrery made by Dr Rittenhouse of Philadelphia. He determined to see it, and accordingly set off on his Journey for that City. When he had got half way, the thought came into his Mind, that if he should find that Dr Rittenhouse had adopted the same principles with himself, that he should loose the Credit of originality in what he had done. He therefore, without farther hesitation, returned & finished what he had begun, which turned out totally different from that of Philadelphia.[107]

We returned to Boston, leaving Miss Binney to return to Water Town. The Afternoon being very clear, and the declining Sun, gilding the distant Hills in a beautiful manner, rendered the prospect on every hand, as we passed thro West Boston, a short distance from the Bridge, very picturesque & agreeable. The grand appearance of Charles River, with the expanded Bay—the Hills forming more than half a Circle, from the West of Roxbury (around the Town over the Neck, Boston & Charles Town) almost to Cambridge, all appearing to be studded with Gentlemen's Seats & Churches, with Spires,—two highly finished Bridges with Lamps, with the Vessels under Sail on the

[107] This was Harvard's third orrery. The first recorded orrery in America was made in England and presented to Harvard by Thomas Hollis of London in 1732; it was destroyed in the fire of 1764. A fine brass orrery made in London by Benjamin Martin was presented to the college by James Bowdoin, and reached Cambridge in 1767. Joseph Pope of Boston, "mathematician, watch-maker and mechanical genius," was the maker of the orrery referred to by Boudinot. Harvard obtained the funds for its purchase by a lottery authorized by the General Court 21 November 1788 and drawn the following March. Pope received £450 for the instrument. The Martin and Pope orreries may still be seen in Cambridge; they are described and illustrated in I. Bernard Cohen, *Some Early Tools of American Science* (Cambridge, 1950). For an account of David Rittenhouse and his famous orrery which was purchased by the College of New Jersey and set up at Nassau Hall in April 1771, see Howard Crosby Rice Jr., *The Rittenhouse Orrery* (Princeton, 1954).

Water, really gave the most prepossessing Ideas of the Towns of Boston & Charles Town, with the Country adjacent. Spent the Evening with Mr Otis the elder,[108] with a large tho select Company.

JULY 29 returned Visits, Dined at Brooklyne with Mr Babcock. Company Mr Gore and several other Gentlemen, and some Ladies.

JULY 30 SUNDAY. Attended Mr Channing's Church in the Morning—a serious solemn Preacher to an apparently devout Congregation.[109] Dined at Mr Higginson Junrs at a Sunday Dinner, and in the afternoon heard Mr Lowel (Son of my old acquaintance Judge Lowel)[110] a sensible fervent Preacher—a very handsome Church & elegant Pulpit, but without a sounding Board, which I take to be a great mistake, and will prove the means of the death of many a Clergyman, as well as prevent the People hearing so well. I am convinced that we, in the middle States, have been greatly decieved with regard to the religious Characters of the Clergy & people of Boston.[111] I went there,

[108] Samuel Allyne Otis (Harvard 1759), Boston merchant and father of Harrison Gray Otis, was active in Revolutionary affairs and served in the Massachusetts house of representatives. He was a delegate to the Continental Congress, and became the first secretary of the U.S. Senate.

[109] The meeting-house in Long Lane was used for the Massachusetts convention of 1788 which ratified the U.S. Constitution; thereafter it was known as the Federal Street Church. William Ellery Channing (Harvard 1798) was minister from 1803 until his death in 1842. A decade was to pass before Channing's famous sermon, preached at the ordination of Jared Sparks at Baltimore in 1819, made him the leader of the Unitarian movement.

[110] Charles Lowell (Harvard 1800) was minister of the West Church (Unitarian) from 1806 to 1861. He was the son of Judge John Lowell (Harvard 1760), who had sat in the Continental Congress with Boudinot, and the father of Robert Traill Spence Lowell (Harvard 1833), missionary in Newfoundland, writer, and Episcopal clergyman; and of James Russell Lowell (Harvard 1838). The West Church on Cambridge Street, built in 1806, is now used as a public library. A photograph of the interior taken about 1875 (Old-Time New England, XX, 165) reveals no sounding-board.

[111] By 1809 all the Congregational churches in Boston but one (the Old South) had given up Calvinist and Trinitarian doctrine, and the ministers of that city and other communities along the coast were preaching a variety

with a full perswasion that most of the Ministers were Socinians, and did not believe in the divinity of the Saviour. I heard nothing like this from the Pulpit. All their Prayers, are remarkable for the repitition, of asking in the name of Christ and for his sake. They generally conclude by giving Praise forever to the Saviour. While I was at Boston, I never heard a doctrine advanced in the Pulpit, that I could not have subscribed to. Indeed the Sermons I heard, were universally practical. The Sacrament of the Lords Supper was administered in a very solemn Manner, and thanks given to God, for the many proofs of the Saviours divinity arising from his death & resurrection. This surprised me greatly. On conversing with a principal Gentleman of the Congregation, I found the great difference of opinion between their principal Ministers & us, lay in their denial of the *total* depravity of Man, and the equality of the Father & the Son. He observed that he could not avoid thinking that we Trinitarians in substance held in three Gods instead of one. I observed to him that he well knew that this was universally denied by us, we being rigidly attached to the unity of the Godhead. I was surprized to find, that he seemed to have no suspicion, that holding the Divinity of the Saviour, and his inequality with the Father, necessarily included the Being of two Gods, and of Course excluded the Idea of Unity, which they all profess to believe equally with us. Being much puzzled to reconcile what appeared to me difficult to account for, I stated my difficulties to an orthodox Minister occasionally in Boston. He told me, if I conversed with the Clergy, they would explain it, by applying the divinity of Christ, to that of his Commission from the Father, and not of his Person. But nevertheless, whatever may be the private opinion of the Ministers, you hear noth-

---

of liberal beliefs and principles later assembled under the name of Unitarianism. The "Boston religion" was at a stage in which liberalism was advancing silently, and if Boudinot heard neither violent heresy nor old-time orthodoxy it was because these clergymen were simply omitting such topics from public discussion.

ing of these doctrines from the pulpits—at least I did not—and altho' I doubt not the truth of my information, as to the opinions of the Clergy & principal People of the Congregations; yet I am convinced that the people at large, consider their Ministers as perfectly Orthodox. I drew this Conclusion from my conversation with Individuals. I was observing, to one of them, that from a Book I had seen in the family, that I feared from such insidious measures as the spreading such Books about, the young People might be led to deny the doctrine of the Saviour's Divinity & Atonement. I was answered with great Earnestness, that if I had been at Church the Sabbath before, I could have no fear on that head, for Mr——had preached a Sermon on that subject, and adduced so many unanswerable proofs from the Scriptures to confirm that doctrine, that no one could doubt for a Moment. Altho I knew that the Minister referred to, was known to hold a different opinion, I did [not] choose to say more on the Subject, lest I should lessen confidence in him, as I was conscious, that it was not believed by the People at large. I must also, in Justice to the People of Boston, acknowledge that the Lords day is more apparently honoured than with us. The Churches are universally Crowded—All ranks, from the highest to the lowest, attend public Worship twice a day.—All dine regularly at one oClock—There is no visiting on that sacred day —and I must add, that a great Spirit of Brotherly love & bearing with each other under differing Sentiments, & opinions, appears to me to prevail among them. An extraordinary Spirit of liberality & unbounded Charity, seems to prevail among all orders of the Inhabitants. Their public Institutions of Charity & usefulness are very numerous, and the Christian Virtues seem to abound among them. Neither profane Swearing or Drunkenness, prevail among the lower ranks of the people, as they do with us. I wish I could say that they did not prevail at all.

JULY 31 MONDAY. This Morning, having previously arranged every thing for the purpose, we sett off for Portsmouth

—passed Charles Town Bridge of about fifteen hundred feet long and 43 broad with 40 lamps and was much pleased to see so handsome a City, reviving from the Ashes of the former Town. Every House was burned by the British in 1775, except two, which had accidentally escaped, and were afterwards burned by our own people. The destruction of this Town was wanton & unnecessary, and only tended to enrage & exasperate the Inhabitants. I cannot well help, repeating a Story I had from a Gentleman of considerable standing in Boston. A fine large Church was among those destroyed in Charles Town. After the Capture of Genll Burgoyne, he had an elegant House assigned him in Cambridge for his residence.[112] An old Deacon of this Church, who after being burned out, had removed about 20 Miles, sometime after Genll Burgoyne was settled at Cambridge, saddled up his old Mare, and rode to Cambridge; going to Genll Burgoyne's House and demanding to see the General, he ordered him admittance. He was introduced into the room where the General was, accompanied by a number of his Officers. He requested to see General Burgoyne. The General was pointed out to him. He then said, and this is General Burgoyne. The Genll answered it was. The old Man raised both his hands, and said I thank my God that I thus see you here; made his bow, & retired. All the Company being greatly surprized at this odd behaviour in an old Countryman, the General sent an aid du Camp out after him, to obtain an explanation of his Conduct. The aid found him mounting his old Mare, and requested to know the meaning of his Conduct. The old Gentleman answered—Why General Burgoyne burned down my Church in

[112] Gentleman Johnny and his staff were quartered in the Henry Vassall house (now 94 Brattle Street) on their way back to Britain following the surrender at Saratoga. The history of this house, which should not be confused with the more famous Major John Vassall-Andrew Craigie-H. W. Longfellow house at 105 Brattle Street, is fully told, along with the story of the passive resistance of Cambridge residents to Burgoyne and the Convention Troops, in Samuel Francis Batchelder, *Bits of Cambridge History* (Cambridge, 1930).

Charlestown in the Year 1775, and God has rewarded him according to his Deeds, and I wanted to see it with my own Eyes, and now I return home quite satisfied.

Charles Town, as a Town, has gained much by its Misfortunes. It is now handsomely rebuilt & greatly enlarged. Not even a trace of its sufferings appear to me to remain. It has at least 300 Houses, chiefly built of Brick.—the Streets are streightened & enlarged—the Churches better built—The public buildings more elegant, and contains about 2000 Inhabitants.

After leaving Charles Town, there is almost a continued line of Houses along the Road, till you come to Malden Bridge over Mystic River at 2 Miles distance. This Bridge is about 600 yards long, the Village contains a considerable number of Houses. A little from this, you ride thro' an unimproved Meadow or low lands filled with Shrubbery on either hand. The Road good & streight—Soil sandy & poor.

We were advised to leave the Turnpike & take the old Road, as the turnpike ran thro' a very unsettled Country. This we repented of, as it lengthened the distance to Salem five Miles. At 3 Miles farther the Country became very rough & hilly to our left, while on our right, was a vast tract of Salt Meadow to the Sea. The road runing at the very foot of the Hills, was very good, being pretty level at the very head of the Meadows. At about 6 Miles from Charles Town, the Country began to change for the better, tho' a rocky barren Craggy Hill to our left at a small distance, quite to Lynn, at 10 Miles from Charles Town. This Town consists of near 200 Houses, and is famous for its Shoe Manufactory. Every House seems to have a small Shoemakers Shop as an appendage to it. In this Town it is said that they make about 200,000 pair per annum, chiefly Womens Stuff & Silk Shoes. From this to Salem is a very romantic Country. It changes for the better, all at once, after passing a long Lake, that affords a beautiful addition to the prospect from the Houses at its head. The Country well settled, till you come to Danvers

at the entry into Salem.[113] This is a Town so entirely connected
with Salem, that the Streets run regularly into it, without any
apparent distinction between them. Danvers contains about 700
Houses, and 4000 Souls & 3 Churches. Salem at 13 Miles distance from Boston on the Turnpike road, is a very large Sea
Port Town, well built & carries on a very large foreign Trade.
It has about 2000 Houses & 12000 Souls. It is the oldest Town
in the State, except Plymouth; and was settled as early as 1628
by Mr [John] Endicott, who was afterwards chosen Governor.
Its Harbour, tho good, is not equal to Boston. It has about
35000 Tons of Topsail Vessels, and about 5000 Tons of fishing
Vessels. In this Town, for about a Mile & an half, the Houses
are as close built as in the City of Philadelphia. There are 9
or 10 well looking Churches with Steeples, one of which serves
as an excellent directory to Sailors entering the Harbour—An
Elegant Town House—a Bank and a number of public & private School Houses. It continues well built to Beverly, which
is separated from Salem, only by a Bridge 96 Rods long—from
which the Street continues as before for 1 1/2 Mile, so that
from the West Entrance into Danvers, thro' Salem & Beverly,
there is one continued Town of five miles long—and I suppose
consists of full 3000 Houses & 20000 Souls. There are a considerable number of very elegant dwelling Houses, richly ornamented with Court Yards & out Houses & handsome Gardens.
I could have no Idea of the rapid improvement of this Country
since I was here, notwithstanding the ravages of an Eight Years
War. As we passed thro Beverly, we saw in several places, the
Stages for drying Codfish, as they carry on a great Trade in this
their Staple. Each fishing Vessel produces annually from 6 to
700 Quintals of fish—4 Churches—At 4 Miles from this, South-
ward on the Sea Shore, lies Marble Head (or as it should be
called, Marvel Head, so named from its original owner).[114]

[113] The south parish of Danvers, through which the Boudinots drove,
became Peabody in 1868.
[114] The histories of Marblehead throw no light on Boudinot's parenthetical

This Town is a perfect Curiosity, from its romantic Situation, being built among a parcel of craggy Rocks, where no person, at first sight, could hardly have thought it possible to have built a House. There was originally scarce Earth enough in the whole Town to form a Garden of half an Acre. There are a few good Houses, built in a hollow between the Rocks, at a great Expence. In the whole Town including every kind of House, there are about 600 and 4 or 5000 Inhabitants, the Men chiefly Fishermen—a very fine Harbour, within a Mile of the open Ocean. It has about 70 Sail of fishing Vessels & 30 Sail of Merchant Men. This Town suffered greatly by the War, and being considerably deserted by its Inhabitants, was reduced almost to an entire ruin. It is just begining to raise its head and it is expected will soon flourish exceedingly. Here are 2 Congr. & one Episcopal Churches & one Methodist. At 7 Miles we came to Wenham, having passed along a beautifull Lake of the same Name, about three Miles in Circumference. We dined here, and then called on the Honble Coll Pickering,[115] who lives within sight of the Tavern. Here we staid all night. This is a fine farm & in a Good State of Cultivation. We enjoyed ourselves much. A select Company awaited our Arrival, and we spent a very agreeable afternoon and Evening. The Coll. is a Man of so much Information and sterling Integrity, that we could not be otherwise than highly entertained. He has been a chosen Character during our revolutionary War;[116] and an able Statesman

---

statement. The Reverend Francis Higginson of Salem wrote in 1629 of the granite headlands which line the shore as "Marble Stone, that we have great rocks of it, and a harbor hard by. Our plantation is from thence called Marble-Harbor." Samuel Roads Jr., *The History and Traditions of Marblehead* (Boston, 1880), 7.

[115] Present-day historians do not employ the same superlatives in writing of Timothy Pickering (Harvard 1763), whose career embraced much valuable and devoted service to his country, but was marred by incredibly harsh and narrow partisanship. Pickering was not above intriguing against President Adams while a member of his cabinet, from which he was summarily dismissed as Secretary of State in May 1800.

[116] He was adjutant general of the Army, with General Washington a long time. (*E.B. note.*)

ever since. He has filled the 1st Stations, as Post Master General, Secretary of War, & Secretary of State, with great Honor, strict Integrity and unblemished reputation. He has been several Years, a Senator of the United States. He has filled this high Station, with great Celebrity and special usefulness to his Country. He has a charming & amiable family, and lives in great Comfort.

AUGUST 1 TUESDAY. Proceeded on our Journey, and at 6 Miles passed Ipswich. This is a considerable Town of about 250 Houses, which appear substantial & comfortable—3 large Churches 1 Baptist & a large Town House, being a County Town. The roads are level & good & the Country well settled. At 4 Miles farther we came to Rowley; about 2 Miles, Lands level & good.—afterwards hilly & Broken, but roads good. This little Town has about 60 or 70 Houses, a Church & a School House. At 2 Miles farther, came into Newbury turnpike. The Country grows very broken & rough, but the roads continue very good. A large tract of Salt Meadow to the right, but very hilly on the left. Came to a handsome Bridge of about 80 yds long—Then another tract of Salt Meadow—Then we passed thro' low level land. Afterwards, 2 Miles rough & barren, till within one Mile of Newbury Port. Saw 2 Steeples on our right & left, and 2 in front. The Entrance into the Town is up a Hill thick planted with 2 Rows of Lombardy Poplars. Put up at a very large elegant Tavern kept by a Mr Coburn. This Town has greatly increased since I saw it. It is situated on the Southerly side of Merimack River 45 Miles East of Boston, and up the River, 2 Miles from the Sea. There are really two Towns united, Newbury & Newbury Port. I speak of the united Towns. There are about 1000 Houses and about 10,000 Inhabitants. They have 13 Churches—1 Episcopal, 8 Congregational, 3 Presbyterian, and one Baptist—an Elegant Town House, a Bank—Insurance Companies, and about 150 Vessels belonging to the port & 2 large School Houses. After dinner, proceeded towards Portsmouth. As we passed thro High Street, our attention was arrested, by what appeared at first sight rather unaccountable. In the Court Yard, to a good looking Tavern, there appeared about 20 Men well dressed, many in uniforms, standing on as many Columns about 12 or 15 feet high. On halting to know the meaning of this appearance, we found them carved Images, exceedingly well done and well painted; as Genlls Washington, Greene & Knox—[Benjamin] Lincoln, Hamilton, Mr Adams, Govr Langdon Dr Franklin & others. Also 4 large Lyons & a Lamb. We were told that a Mr Dexter[117] had suddenly risen from very low Circumstances, to a considerable Fortune by speculation—that it turned his Brain:—and that among many other frantic Tricks, this was one of his performances. He thought his plain wife not polite enough for him, and he tempted her to separate from him & return to her Father, by a considerable Sum of money. He then purchased a Carriage & four Horses & went among the Young Ladies of the Country, to seek another Wife. He soon found that he was made a laughing stock wherever he went. He got tired of his new mode of Life. He made application to his old fashioned

---

[117] Timothy Dexter (1747-1806) is one Yankee who is not going to be forgotten. He came from an indigent family, had little schooling, and followed the trade of leather-dressing in Newburyport. He married a widow (Elizabeth Lord Frothingham) with a little money, and with this and his own accumulations he bought up great quantities of depreciated Continental currency. When the government adopted the policy of funding and assumption in 1791, Dexter became a wealthy man, able to indulge his vanities and eccentricities, one of which was to call himself Lord Timothy. In 1796 he purchased the Jonathan Jackson mansion on High Street and had a ship-carver make more than forty life-sized wooden statues, realistically painted, of great men—and one of himself. He employed an ex-fish-peddler as poet laureate to compose odes in his honor, and he himself wrote *A Pickle for the Knowing Ones*, innocent of punctuation except at the end, where there was a page of "stops" for the reader to distribute as he pleased. Legends of Dexter abound, many of which he fostered; it was part of his shrewdness to play the fool, and it is known that although he drank heavily and inveterately he always transacted his business in the morning when he was sober. One of J. P. Marquand's early books is an amusing biography of *Lord Timothy Dexter* (New York, 1925).

wife, to return to him, and she had wit enough to insist on another handsome Sum, before she would comply. Dexter had lately died. The House is let to a Mr Richardson as a Tavern, who keeps up the group of Images, in hopes of drawing Custom from the Curious. At 1 Mile passed 2 large Covered Bridges over Merimack River, separated by a small Island, and then entered New Hampshire. At 2 Miles passed thro' Salisbury. This is a Village of about 200 Houses, surrounding a large Bay. Here they carry on Ship building. They have 2 Churches & a large School House. A few Miles farther we passed another large Church and at 5 Miles came to Hampton, where there is a Church & some good Houses. At 3 Miles farther North Hill or North Hampton. The Road rather rough & Country uncultivated till near the Town. Entered it over a fine Causeway made at Considerable Expence. At 5 Miles farther we Came to Greenland—the Country continues rather rough & unimproved, and roads good but hilly, much in the state it was 40 years ago—no sensible alteration. The grain very small Ears, and even the Timothy Grass, is but half the usual size. We passed 3 Churches in different places on the road. The Houses are very thinly scattered over the Country. At 4 Miles farther the Country begins to change—puts on an appearance of better Cultivation—fine Meadows & good Grain. About 2 Miles farther, Land stony, broken & barren; but good roads quite to Portsmouth. We entered it just before Sunset, and were received by our friend Govr Langdon & family with great Joy. He had just returned from a ride to meet us, but thought we had failed in coming.

Mr Langdon[118] is a Gentleman who has been famous for the

---

[118] John Langdon (1741-1819) was a member of the Continental Congress in 1775 and 1776, returning to Portsmouth as Navy agent to superintend the construction of ships of war. He served several times as speaker of the state house of representatives, and in 1777 he staked his fortune to equip the brigade of General John Stark which defeated the Hessians at Bennington. Later he was a member of the Constitutional Convention of 1787, and was twice elected to the U.S. Senate, serving as first president *pro tempore* in April 1789 when the electoral votes were counted. Langdon had

part he has taken in the late American revolution. He originally commanded a Merchant Vessel out of Portsmouth in the London Trade. By his soft manners & amiable Conduct to Passengers, with the strictest integrity in his mercantile transactions, he soon became an object of attention with the Merchants & Passengers, and thereby accumulated a handsome property, which enabled him to enter into an extensive Trade himself, and he in a few Years, became one of the richest Merchants in Portsmouth. At the begining of the American Troubles with the Mother Country, he took a very active part in favour of his Country, and obtained the Confidence of his fellow Citizens to so great a degree, that he was sent to Congress in 1775 as a representative from New Hampshire. Here he signalized himself, as warmly attached to prudent, tho' energetic Measures to obtain the redress of our grievances. When Congress determined to establish a Navy, the building a 74 Gun Ship at Portsmouth was committed to his Agency & Superintendance. This he executed in the best manner, and when finished, Congress being unable to fit her out, she was presented, as an act of gratitude & respect, to the King of France, in return for the many favours we had received from him.[119] When the new Constitution was formed, Mr Langdon was sent a Senator from his State, where he acquitted himself to general acceptation. He was Chairman of the Committee of both Houses, who were sent to Elizabeth Town in New Jersey, to recieve General Washington, then lately chosen President of the United States, and to conduct him to New York. He was considered as a Warm federalist, and entered into all the Measures of the new ad-

---

finally retired from public life just before Boudinot's visit and was living in the Portsmouth mansion where he had entertained Washington and other distinguished men; this house is now a museum of the Society for the Preservation of New England Antiquities.

[119] This was the *America*, launched 5 November 1782. The French renamed her *Impétueux*, but the British captured the ship from them in the "Battle of the First of June" (1794).

ministration. He very highly esteemed our new President, and placed great confidence in his Integrity & Prudence. Being a thorough American he became offended with some unguarded expressions which fell from Mr Adams, the then Vice President relative to the nature of the most eligible system of Government for this Country;[120] which sowred his Mind against him, so that when Mr Adams was raised to the presidential Chair, Mr Langdon easily fell into the Snares laid for him by the opposition to Government, and he entered into their Views & measures, which soon estranged him from most of his old Friends. After this he lived, while at Congress, very retired, and kept but little Company. As he had not had the advantages of an Education, and being a very gentlemanly Man, of amiable Manners & mild deportment, he did not altogether suit the violent Party he had connected himself with. They rather neglected him, and after encouraging him to hope for the Vice Presidency, they left him in the lurch & preferred Coll Burr, as a more energetic & decided Character, who, they expected, would go all lengths with them, not regarding Consequences. After this he retired to his domestic Circle.

But he was soon again called to active & public life. His fellow Citizens chose him Governor of the State, which, with the exception of a few Years, he has administered ever since, till the last Year, when he was left out and a Federalist chosen in his room. He has lately wholly changed his Character & Conduct. From a perfect Man of the World, and regarding only earthly things, he has undergone a thorough change of Heart & Temper, and become a serious and exemplary professor of Evangelical religion. He seems to maintain this Character with great

[120] In a conversation with Adams early in 1793, Langdon had referred somewhat tactlessly to the number of votes George Clinton, the Republican, had received in the recent presidential election. Adams exclaimed: "Damn 'em, damn 'em, damn 'em. You see that an elective government will not do." Langdon's shift to Jeffersonianism is fully explained in Lawrence Shaw Mayo, *John Langdon of New Hampshire* (1937), Chap. XX.

sincerity and unostentatious piety. I was exceedingly pleased to see so happy a Contrast to his former Conduct, and delighted to find that his Lady & Sister were listed in the same Glorious Cause.[121]

AUGUST 2 WEDNESDAY. Dined at Mr Langdons with Coll. Whipple,[122] Judge Sherburne,[123] the Revd Mr & Miss Buxminster,[124] Mr Elwen & Lady (Daughter & only Child of Mr Langdon)[125] & Capt Walbeck[126] Commandant of the fort. The

[121] In 1806 at the age of sixty-five John Langdon became a member of the North Church at Portsmouth, together with his wife, Elizabeth Sherburne Langdon, and his sister Elizabeth, the widow of Colborn Barrell.

[122] Colonel Joseph Whipple (1737-1816) was in middle life a pioneer settler of the township of Jefferson, New Hampshire, the entire acreage of which he at one time owned; he was later port collector at Portsmouth by appointment of Presidents Washington and Jefferson. New Hampshire Hist. Soc. *Proceedings*, III, 289-320.

[123] John Samuel Sherburne (Dartmouth 1776) was the brother of Mrs. Langdon and had lost a leg in the Battle of Butts Hill, Rhode Island, in 1778. He practiced law in Portsmouth until he was made U.S. district attorney for New Hampshire by President Jefferson; subsequently he was U.S. district judge for that state.

[124] Joseph Buckminster (Yale 1770) had been pastor of the North Church in Portsmouth since 1779. He was the father of Joseph Stevens Buckminster, whose adoption of Unitarian beliefs had been a bitter disappointment to him. The Miss Buckminster mentioned was either his eldest daughter Lucy Maria, who married Professor John Farrar of Harvard, or Eliza, who married Thomas Lee of Brookline and became a prolific author. Her *Memoirs of Rev. Joseph Buckminster, D.D., and of his son Rev. Joseph Stevens Buckminster* (1851) was praised by Carlyle as revealing to him the highest aspect of New England character.

[125] Thomas Elwyn Jr. of Canterbury, Kent, was matriculated at Trinity College, Oxford, in 1792. He came to America in 1796 and after completing a tour he read law in Philadelphia, where he met and fell in love with the beautiful Betsey Langdon, daughter of Senator Langdon. It was not easy for the old Revolutionary patriot to give his daughter to a British subject, but he did, and the marriage was a very happy one. The three sons who went to Harvard hyphenated their name as Langdon-Elwyn.

[126] John de Barth Walbach, Baron de Walbach (1766-1857), had been an officer in the service of both France and Germany before coming to Philadelphia on a visit in 1798. Circumstances compelled him to remain in this country, and he had a long and notable career in the U.S. Army, rising to the rank of brevet brigadier-general in 1850. At this time he was stationed

Revd Mr Buxminster is an able, well read Divine. His truly pious & evangelical Character and demeanor as a Gospel Minister, greatly endears him to his People. He appears to me to be an Israelite in whom there is no guile. He is laborious in his calling, a faithful, active & zealous Minister of the Salvation of Jesus Christ. He is about 55 Years of age—Modest, humble & exemplary.

AUGUST 3 THURSDAY. In the morning Visited the different parts of the Town & then dined at home, with Mr Buxminster, Mr & Mrs Elwin. Mrs Barrel a worthy excellent widow Lady & Sister to Mr Langdon, lives with him, and always made our parties agreeable. After Dinner we rode out to Mr Elwyn's Farm and drank Tea. The road to it thro' a fine improved Country, about the distance from Portsmouth, of about three or four Miles. Returned in the Evening & attended a Lecture at Mr Buxminsters Church. He grows in our Esteem.

AUGUST 4 FRIDAY. We rode this morning to the Bridge over Piscataway River to the Province of Main, at Six Miles from Portsmouth. The River here divides into 4 Branches. The Easternmost runs to Berwick. The next to Dover. The Northern to Durham and the western to Exeter. The Bridge is divided in the middle by a small Island of about 3 Acres. Is 452 feet long. The Water is 50 feet deep at low Water at the Bridge —a little on one side it is 70 feet deep.

Portsmouth is a genteel well built Town, containing about 1000 Houses—a considerable number elegant and well built. About 7 or 8000 Inhabitants—an elegant Town House—Eight large Churches one of them an Episcopal, a Baptist, a Universalist & a Methodist Church. They have also a large Accademy and 7 or 8 public or free Schools for Boys & 2 for Girls, besides a number of large private Schools. Here are also three

---

at Fort Constitution on New Castle Island in Portsmouth Harbor. C. K. Gardner, *Dictionary of . . . the Army of the United States* (1860), 465; *Appleton's Cyc. Amer. Biog.*, VI, 319.

Specie Banks & two Insurance Companies. Portsmouth has one
of the finest Harbours in the Union. a Ship of 74 Guns was built
on an Island a little above the Town. It never freezes here, so
that Vessels go & come all Winter without interruption from
Ice. Mr Langdon informs me that, he never knew a Vessel
detained 6 Hours by the Ice in his life. There about one hundred Sail of Square rigged Vessels, besides a large number of
Coasters & Fishermen belonging to the Port. From a lofty Hill
there appeared 12 or 14 Islands in the Harbour. The Village
of New Castle is built on one of them.

AUGUST 4 FRIDAY. About 12 oClock we took an affecting leave
of our Friends, and sett off on our return for Boston. Mr & Mrs
Langdon & Mr & Miss Buxminster accompanied us about Six
Miles on our Way. We stopped & dined with Mr Elwyn who
joined our party. At Greenland, we left our Friends, and taking
the road to the right, soon passed thro' Spaham [Stratham],
a small Town of 40 or 50 Houses & a large Church. From
thence along good roads, but an indifferently improved Country, we came at 15 Miles distance from Portsmouth, to Exeter,
where we lodged at a Mr Deans, who with his Lady waited on
us at the Tavern, & finding the Tavern thronged, insisted on
our taking a Bed with them. The Country around this Town
appears better Cultivated & very pleasant. About 300 Houses,
a large handsome Accademy under a Mr Abbot, a Gentleman of
excellent Character.[127] The Governor of the State lives here,[128]

[127] Boudinot makes this sound like the typical "Accademy" he saw in nearly
every town he went through, but these were locally supported and most of
them later became high schools. Phillips Exeter Academy was founded in 1781
by a member of the same family that founded Phillips Academy at Andover
and has become one of the ranking secondary schools of America. In 1809
the school was housed in a fine Georgian structure with a belfry, which had
been built in 1794, and was destroyed by fire in 1870. Benjamin Abbot was
graduated from Harvard in 1788, became principal of Exeter the same year,
and for half a century conducted the school with a firm hand and with
enthusiasm for the classics and for accurate and thorough scholarship. When
he retired in 1838 he could count among his boys Lewis Cass, J. S. Buckminster, Edward Everett, Jared Sparks, John Adams Dix, George Bancroft,

and there is some Trade carried on, the river being navigable to this place. There are 3 Churches one a Baptist, a Bank, a large Court House and about 1800 to 2000 Inhabitants.

AUGUST 5 SATURDAY. Set off early in the Morning. At 6 Miles came to Kingston a small Town with a Church—a fine, well cultivated broken Country. At 12 Miles farther, thro' a good Country but rather hilly, we stopped at Haverhill on the Marroneck [Merrimack] River & navigable, being about 12 Miles above Newbury Port. This is a considerable Town, well built, with a large Church & about 150 Houses, many of them make a very good appearance, and many of the Stores seem to be fire proof. After resting some time, we passed a large, well built wooden bridge on stone Piers, with 5 Arches & Bents, over the River. On the West side, rose a high Hill, from which we had a grand prospect of the River & adjacent Country. We immediately entered Bradford, a long scattered Village, well cultivated & Scenery beautiful. At Eight Miles from Haveril, we came to Andover. Here we had a pleasant meeting with our old Friends Dr Edward D Griffin & Lady.[129] After Dining with

---

and Daniel Webster, who made one of his most felicitous speeches on that occasion. Laurence M. Crosbie, *The Phillips Exeter Academy* (Exeter, 1923).

[128] Jeremiah Smith (Rutgers 1780) was then serving his single term as governor. He had been chief justice of the superior court of New Hampshire, and afterward returned to that post.

[129] Edward Dorr Griffin (Yale 1790) was a great big man, six feet three in height and built in proportion, with a voice "of immense compass, and peculiarly melodious and solemn," who was always getting into trouble. Boudinot had known him at the First Presbyterian Church at New Ark. At Andover his ambitions and extravagance were vexing to the simple Puritan community, and he soon resigned. At the Park Street Church he refused to meet with the Boston Association of Ministers and he made himself obnoxious at Harvard where he tried unsuccessfully to force his way into a reluctant Board of Overseers as an *ex officio* member. When the Park Street Church finances became shaky, he went back to New Ark to a newly-founded Second Presbyterian Church; there his opponents affronted him by a salary cut. In 1821 he became president of Williams College, then languishing and losing students to its new neighbor, Amherst. Griffin built up the college and gained for it such a high reputation for teaching and discipline that parents soon

them, the Doctor was obliged to leave us, as he was previously engaged to preach at Milton beyond Boston. He prevailed on us to promise to stay on Monday, when he would join us again. Dr Griffin was lately removed from New Ark in New Jersey, being chosen a Professor of pulpit Eloquence in the Theological Seminary or College in this place. He is also to preach 4 Months during the Winter & Spring to the Calvinist Church in Boston.[130] This is a new & elegant Church, not yet quite finished, opposite the Mall in Boston. Great opposition has been made to him there, by the other Denominations, principally on account of his being a zealous Calvinist. This has been increased by the propagation of the most gross Calumnies & Falsehoods that have been reported concerning him. Many of which I have industriously contradicted, from my own Knowledge. He is a sensible, learned, well read, able Divine—an excellent Preacher, but perhaps too warm & a little dogmatical in urging his particular Tenets, but which I doubt not proceeds from a thorough conviction that they are necessary to Salvation. However, as he has been warned of the ground on which he will stand, and being a prudent Man, I have no hesitation in concluding that he will make his way good, and finally be acceptable to the Majority of the People. The Revd Dr Pearson the Professor of [Sacred Literature] & Lady waited on us.[131] This Gentleman

---

filled it up with their unmanageable sons, and the president was in trouble again. He resigned in 1836 and left Williams in the capable hands of Mark Hopkins.

Dr. Griffin's Lady was Frances Huntington of Coventry, Connecticut.

[130] The Park Street Church, still a conspicuous and handsome landmark, was built in 1809-10. Its organization in February 1809 was one of the incidents in what Evarts Boutell Greene called the Puritan Counter-Reformation (American Antiquarian Society *Proceedings*, Apr. 1932), namely the measures taken by the embattled orthodox to combat the rise of Unitarianism.

[131] Eliphalet Pearson (Harvard 1773) had manufactured saltpetre and gunpowder for the Revolutionary army, and was afterward the first principal of Phillips Academy. Later he was Hancock Professor of Hebrew and other Oriental Languages at Harvard and for two years acting president, but left when the university passed him by and elected a Unitarian president and divin-

was for many Years Professor in the College at Cambridge, and is a learned, sensible & polite Man—Seems to be possessed of great Information and his Character stands high for his Theological erudition.

AUGUST 6 SUNDAY. This morning went to the Parish Church and heard an excellent, evangelical & impressive Sermon from the Revd Mr Wood Professor of Theology in the College.[132] He also administered the Sacrament of the Lords Supper to a large number of serious Communicants about 250; we were invited to unite with this band of Brethren & Sisters in the Lord. The Audience was very numerous. It was a solemn day. Mr Wood is a Preacher of the first rate, and supplied the Pulpit this day on account of the Vacancy occasioned by the Sudden death of the late Pastor, Mr French,[133] who suddenly departed about 10 Days ago. He was a pious Minister, much beloved & greatly lamented. Mr Wood preached again in the Afternoon and improved on our hands. He promises to be a burning & shining light in the Church.

There are three young Students in divinity in the House

---

ity professor. He was one of the organizers of Andover Theological Seminary, persuading the Hopkinsians and the moderate Calvinists to bury the hatchet and join forces in the face of the common enemy, Unitarianism, and he held a professorship there for one year, but then retired to engage in farming and literary pursuits. It is reported that he had strong Unitarian leanings in later life. His Lady was Sarah Bromfield.

[132] Leonard Woods (Harvard 1796), sometime minister of West Newbury, Massachusetts, was active in the founding of Andover Seminary, and held the Abbot Professorship of Christian Theology there for thirty-eight years. In 1820-22 he carried on a pamphlet war with Professor Henry Ware of Harvard on the merits of Unitarianism *vs.* Calvinism which was called the "Wood'n Ware Controversy." His wife was Abigail Wheeler, and one of their sons, Leonard Jr. (Union 1807), was president of Bowdoin for many years.

[133] Jonathan French had been a soldier in the French and Indian Wars and a sergeant in the regular army at Castle William, Boston, before entering Harvard College, where he was graduated in 1771 at the age of thirty-one. He was settled over the South Parish of Andover the following year and was minister there until his death, 28 July 1809.

with us: Messrs Cumming, Crane & Conger,[134] all from New Ark who are preparing for the Ministry. They all three discover fine genius & promise fair to become able Ministers of the new Testament.

This Institution[135] originally took its rise from the liberality of the Late Honble Samll & John Philips, Sons of the first Minister of the Parish, who more than 30 Years ago. founded an Accademy in this place "for the promotion of true Piety & Virtue". In 1789 The Honble John Philips gave $20,000 for "the virtuous & pious education of youth of Genius & serious dispositions" in this Accademy. By his last Will, he bequeathed to an Accademy he had also founded in Exeter, two thirds, and to this Institution one third of his Estate, particularly "for the benefit of Charity Scholars, and also for the assistance of Students in divinity, under the direction of some eminent Calvinistic Minister, till an Orthodox Professor of Divinity shall be appointed in one of these Accademies". To this fund was added a Legacy of $4000 by the Honble William Philips of Boston.[136] In 1807 the Trustees of Philips's Accademy applied to the Legislature, and were authorized to hold property to the amount

[134] Hooper Cumming and John Riggs Crane were classmates in Princeton 1805 and both men were graduated in the first Andover class (1810). Dr. Cumming held pastorates in New Ark, Schenectady, Albany, Manhattan, and Charleston, S.C., before his death in 1825. Dr. Crane was pastor at Middletown, Conn., for twenty-five years. Lewis Le Conte Congar (Princeton 1806) died at Andover while a member of the seminary in January 1810.

[135] Phillips Academy at Andover was established in 1778 and has grown and prospered to the present day, though it was overshadowed for a century by the seminary which was engrafted upon it. The founders were Samuel Phillips (Harvard 1734) of Andover and his brother John Phillips (Harvard 1735), resident of Exeter, who was also the founder of Phillips Exeter Academy; they were the sons of Reverend Samuel Phillips (Harvard 1708), first minister of the South Parish of Andover. Claude M. Fuess, *An Old New England School* (Boston, 1917).

[136] The Honorable William Phillips (1722-1804) was a brother of the academy's founders; he was a wealthy Boston merchant and Revolutionary patriot.

of $5000 per annum in addition to their former powers.[137] Soon after this "Phoebe Philips of Andover relict of Samuel Philips Esq late lieut Governor of Massachusets & John Philips Son of the sd Samuel & Phoebe jointly & severally bound themselves to erect & furnish two separate buildings, one of which to be three Stories high [Phillips Hall] & such other dimensions as to furnish convenient lodging Rooms for 50 Students. Another two Stories high, for a Kitchen with private rooms for a Stewards Family—a dining room, a Chapel or Lecture room & a Library Room." Samuel Abbot of Andover aforesaid, also gave $20 000 for maintaining a Professor of Christian Theology & for encouragement of Students in divinity. Some time after this, Moses Brown, William Bartlet of Newbury Port & John Norris of Salem,[138] became associate Founders & added $50 000 to the general Fund, for purposes & on Terms contained in their Instrument of the Donation. The most essential Terms of this Institution is to conduct it after the Principles of the Westminster

[137] This act permitted the establishment of Andover Theological Seminary, which was opened for instruction the following year. The seminary was one of the major undertakings of the orthodox Congregationalists in their efforts to cope with the new liberal Unitarian theology, and was occasioned by Harvard's defection from the old creeds in the appointment of Henry Ware, a Unitarian, as Hollis Professor of Divinity in 1805. So carefully did the projectors of the seminary hedge the institution with trustees, statutes, creeds, restrictions and visitatorial groups that much of its history was marked by theological fracases and heresy trials. Finally, in 1908, its student body reduced and its influence impaired, the seminary—in an action which undoubtedly caused more people to turn over in their graves than any similar event in New England religious history—sold its buildings to Phillips Academy, and affiliated itself with Harvard University.

[138] Samuel Abbot was a wealthy retired Boston merchant living in Andover. Moses Brown had accumulated a large fortune as a chaise-maker. William Bartlet's wealth was amassed in the East India trade. John Norris was a merchant and state senator. The deathbed scene of Norris's widow Mary is recounted with zest by William Bentley, the Unitarian parson of Salem, in his *Diary* (IV, 12f). Four of the local orthodox clergy, hearing of the old lady's imminent end, rushed to her chamber, excluded the relatives, and made her execute a will giving $30,000 to Andover, the same amount for foreign missions, and a thousand dollars to each clergyman present.

shorter Catechism, and the Statutes of the Founders. There are now about 35 Students in this College. It consists of Professors of Natural Theology—Sacred Literature, Ecclesiastical History, Christian Theology & Pulpit Eloquence.

AUGUST 7 MONDAY. Spent this day at Andover. Dr Griffin returned about one oClock. We spent our time with great chearfulness and were highly entertained by the hospitality & agreeable Conversation of the Dr & his Lady, with the young Students. Drank Tea at Mrs Philips with Dr Pearson, Professor Wood & their Ladies, and our Host & Hostess, Mr Farrar[139] &c Mrs Philips is a very agreeable old Lady, and seems to be rejoicing, in the last Stage of life, in the prosperity of her Labours.[140]

AUGUST 8 TUESDAY. This Morning, Mrs Bradford went with Dr Pearson, Professor Wood & their Ladies to view an extraordinary prospect from a very high Hill or Mountain about 1 1/2 Miles from the College.[141] On their return they gave a very captivating Account of this prospect. The Eye takes in a View of about 300 Miles in Circumference, by turning the Head, and affords a full View, inexpressible delightful, of a distant range of Hills, with very large intervals of Land covered with Houses & highly cultivated Fields, large Forests & meandering Waters that, as Mrs B. observed, far surpassed any thing we had seen. On a bright day, 28 Steeples appear in sight. The weather being Hazy, they saw but a few of them. At 2 oClock left our hospitable Friends, being escorted a few Miles by Dr Griffin & Lady. We called on Mr Abbot, one of the founders of the Institution, on our Way, who received us with great

[139] Samuel Farrar (Harvard 1797) was for many years trustee, treasurer, and librarian of Andover Seminary.

[140] Phoebe Foxcroft Phillips, widow of Samuel Phillips Jr. (Harvard 1771), had been devoted to the welfare of the academy boys, and at this time was taking special interest in the erection of Phillips Hall, which she and her son John were donating to the seminary.

[141] Prospect Hill is located about a mile out Salem Street, southeast of Phillips Academy.

politeness. The Turnpike from Andover to Boston (about 20 Miles) is as fine as the One from New Ark to Brunswick.

At about 9 Miles came to a cluster of 6 or 8 Houses and an elegant Tavern, called Stoneham. At about 8 farther we passed thro Medford, a beautiful little Village, remarkably neat & clean. On our way to the South of Stoneham 2 or 3 Miles, saw a beautiful Lake on our left, called Redding or Spot Pond. At a few Miles farther came to a very large Lake, presenting an elegant Sheet of Water, I thought several Miles long, with the appearance of a large Island in the Midst, and a handsome large House on it, tho' it might be a neck of land, connected with the Main. Passed a Causeway over the Meadows of 2 1/2 Miles long a fine Turnpike. This led us to Charles Town & over the Bridge into Boston, where we were welcomed to our former lodgings by our inmates & the Family.

Before I proceed further, I must mention some Facts related to us at Portsmouth, which are worth recording. Early in the 18th Century, Henry Phipps (afterwards Sir Harry Phipps)[142] was one of eight orphan Children, whose Mother lived on Rosee Island in the River Kennebeck in the Province of Main. She was so poor, that they lived principally on Clams & any thing that accidentally turned up. He proposed to his Mother that he should go to Boston & learn a trade, to enable them to live a little better. The Mother thought she could not support the rest of the Children without him. However, she at last Consented. He accordingly went, and in his leisure hours, applied closely to the Study of Navigation. One day he took up a News paper, and his curiosity being raised to read it, he was much

---

[142] Sir William Phips (1650/1-1694/5) is the subject of this moral tale, which is wrong in almost every particular. Phips had risen to be a Boston ship-contractor when he heard from sea-rovers of the vast wealth in sunken Spanish ships. His first venture, financed by Charles II, failed, but the second, backed by the Duke of Albemarle, succeeded in obtaining £300,000, and for this Phips was knighted in 1687. He afterward became High Sheriff of New England and the first royal governor of Massachusetts Bay, but his later activities are far too extensive and involved for one of our footnotes.

taken with an Account of two Spanish Galoons [galleons] which had foundered & sunk in a certain latitude in the West Indies. He immediately formed a plan of enriching himself and whoever should join him in the undertaking, by endeavouring to seek after these Galoons. He communicated his Scheme to some Gentlemen, who being pleased with the ingenuity of this Scheme, supplied him with Money and fitted him out for the purpose. On his first Voyage, he failed in any discovery of his Object, and returned under great disappointment. However he could not give it up, but prevailed on his Friends to aid him in a second Voyage. In this he proved Successful. He found the Vessels, by means of his Divers, and almost loaded his Vessel with Dollars. He went to England with them, and then returned for a third attempt, and again Succeeded. He was then Knighted and made Governor of Massachusets. He purchased the Island where his Mother lived, and it is still called Phipps's Point.

AUGUST 9 WEDNESDAY. Dined at Home, but drank Tea at Brooklyne at Mr Babcocks in company with Mr Gore & Lady.

AUGUST 10 THURSDAY. Was suddenly taken down with a severe fit of the Gout which confined me to my Bed & room till Septr 11th.

During my Confinement, I experienced the most unbounded attention & kindness from all my acquaintance, and from many persons whose Names I had never heard of before. Every thing that I could want, was supplied me—indeed my Friends would not let me feel that I was sick & from home. Govr Gore with Mr Parkman, Mr Sullivan[143] & a number of

---

[143] Christopher Gore (Harvard 1776) had been the first U.S. attorney for the district of Massachusetts and a commissioner under the Jay Treaty in England; he was Governor of Massachusetts in 1809 and later U.S. Senator. He lived in a magnificent house in Waltham, and bequeathed his entire residuary estate to Harvard; the funds were used to build Gore Hall, the college library from 1841 to 1913.

Samuel Parkman (1750-1824) was one of the richest merchants of Boston, and he and his sons were liberal benefactors of Harvard. It was his wealth which enabled his grandson Francis Parkman (Harvard 1844) to devote his life to the writing of American history.

others whose names were not left in Writing called on me repeatedly. I cannot sufficiently express my gratitude for the exceeding hospitality of the Citizens of Boston, particularly Mr Stephen Higginson Junr Mr Babcock Mr George Cabbot & Mr John Gore & their Families.

On the 5th [SEPTEMBER] as a preparative to my going home, I was taken into my Carriage by 2 Men, and in company with Judge Tudor & Miss Hatch,[144] I rode to Mr Craigie's New Toll Bridge.[145] This is a very beautiful piece of Architecture, lately built by Mr Craigie of Cambridge, at his own Expence, over Charles River, in sight of West Boston Bridge, and about the same length & Plan, by which the road to Cambridge is much shortned. These Bridges, with others in the Neighbourhood, appear all to be very well contrived, but as they are all of Wood, they must be liable to decay, and soon will want continual repairs. Altho' the Architecture is good and answers the End for the present compleatly, so as to afford a very low Toll (only one Shilling for a Coachee) yet there are none of them to be compared, to either the Skuylkill or Trenton Bridges, for either durability or Architecture.[146]

The great Boston lawyer James Sullivan, who was in the Continental Congress with Boudinot, had died in 1808; probably the caller was his son William (Harvard 1792) who followed his father's profession.

[144] It is likely that Miss Hatch was the daughter of Boudinot's landlady.

[145] The Craigie, or Canal Bridge, which ran from Leverett Street to Lechmere Point in East Cambridge, was opened to the public on commencement day, 30 August 1809. It was demolished in 1905, and the Charles River Dam now covers the site. The bridge was by no means the disinterested enterprise that Boudinot makes it appear, but part of a huge and modern-sounding real estate speculation which went sour and impoverished Andrew Craigie. The old man's last years were spent virtually as a prisoner in his Brattle Street mansion, from which he emerged only on Sundays when the process-servers were absent. Lucius Robinson Paige, *History of Cambridge, Massachusetts* (Boston, 1877), 203-209; John Holmes on Andrew Craigie in Colonial Society of Massachusetts *Publications*, VII, 403-407.

[146] The Schuylkill Bridge at Philadelphia was opened to travel in 1805 and destroyed by fire in 1875. The Trenton Bridge was finished in 1806 and was

We passed on, to the intersection of the Charles Town Road, and returned by the way of Bunker Hill. We rode up to the field of Battle in 1775. As Judge Tudor was present at that bloody Scene, his information was very gratifying. I could not View this very extraordinary Spot of Ground, without various & strong emotions, it having been, together with Trenton in New Jersey, the most important of the whole War. I can say it from experience, as I saw the effects it produced, in almost every movement of the british Army afterwards. I was once met by some british officers, when I recieved a flag of Truce. One of them behaved a little indecorous by telling me in conversation, that he could not tell whether the Americans had courage to fight or not. That they always kept in the Woods, and never would come out in the plain open Country, that they might know whether they had Courage or not. Not being pleased with his Conversation, I retorted on him, by saying, it arose from fear in the british Troops, who had not the Courage to come into the woods to let us know whether *they* could fight or not. That I wished to know what reason there was, that we should meet regular disciplined Troops in the Plain, more than they should meet our irregular undisciplined Troops in the Woods. That they came to invade us, and therefore it was their business to attack us, where ever they found us. But I wished to know, why with all their Courage, they never went out to forage further than 3 or 4 Miles from the City, and then with a train of Artillery, and 3 or 4 000 Men, while we scoured all along their lines with not more than 100 Men, without artillery & 16 or 17 Miles from our Camp. He suddenly answered, General Howe remembers Bunkers Hill.

I was surprized to find that the general Government had not taken a single measure to perpetuate this very important event by any public Monument on the Spot. The Society of free Ma-

---

replaced by an iron structure in 1875-76. Both bridges rested on large stone piers and had enormous, heavy, and cumbersome wooden spans.

sons have, much to their honor, erected a small monument to the Memory of their Brother General Warren, but the United States have done nothing, worthy a nation, on this memorable occasion, which calls so loudly on our public Councils.[147] Every circumstance of this all important Day, should be authenticated beyond contradiction and the danger of being lost from a lapse of time. Military Men in the Course of a few Years, when they visit this Spot, will never believe the possibility of a faithful narration of the actual Facts that happened on that Day. That an Army so well Commanded as the british Army was at that time, could ever have been guilty of so great a blunder as was committed on that memorable Day. When the Americans were discovered on Breeds Hill, for that is the Name of the Hill, being considerably to the East of Bunkers Hill, they consisted of about 1200 raw undisciplined Militia, without any regular Commander (General Warren being but a Volunteer, and the principal Officer present was Major [   ])[148] armed with the common Guns & fowling Pieces of the Country and a few Rifles;

[147] The monument Boudinot inspected was a square 18-foot Tuscan column on a base which King Solomon's Lodge of Charlestown had erected as a memorial to General Joseph Warren in 1794. The existing Bunker Hill Monument was begun in 1825 and completed and dedicated in 1843. The "principal originators" of the monument were William Tudor Jr., editor of the *North American Review* and son of Boudinot's cicerone; Dr. John Collins Warren, nephew of General Warren; Professor Edward Everett, Thomas Handasyd Perkins, and Daniel Webster; they, with others, were incorporated as the Bunker Hill Monument Association in 1823, which raised the funds for the 220-foot Quincy granite structure from private sources.

[148] On the command at Bunker Hill, John Pitts, Bostonian and member of the Provincial Congress, wrote from Watertown to Samuel Adams 20 July 1775: "To be plain it appears to me there never was more confusion and less command. No one appeard to have any but Col. [William] Prescott whose bravery can never be enough acknowledged and applauded.—General Putnam was employd in collecting the men but there were not officers to lead them on." Quoted from the MS letter in the New York Public Library by Allen French in *The First Year of the American Revolution* (Boston, 1934), 228-229; Mr. French concludes: "That most of the hesitating officers had neither knowledge or authority, and that Prescott commanded in the redoubt, is all we need to add."

but no Bayonets to signify any thing. Perhaps there was not a dozen Guns of the same Caliber. Their Ammunition was so trifling, that it was plain they did not expect any very serious Conflict. Their Artillery consisted of 2 or 3 small field pieces, but they had neither Provision or Drink. This Hill and the Lands surrounding it, including Charles Town, is a kind of promontory running out from the Main, into Charles River & the Bay, and connected with it, by means of a narrow Neck or Isthmus of about 2 or 300 Yards wide, on the Northwest of the promontory. Over this Neck those hardy New England Men had thus imprudently ventured at the risque of their lives, without making the least provision for covering their retreat, in case of necessity. On the Field of Battle they had no other artificial protection, than a common Post & rail fence that divided the Field, to which they removed another, that was near at hand, within 4 or 5 feet. Between these they filled in a few Cocks of Grass that were accidentally in the place making into Hay. Behind this, they lay on the ground waiting an attack. The British Commander, Genll [Thomas] Gage, instead of sending the detachment to the aforesaid narrow neck of land, and drawing a line of 3 or 400 Men, with a few pieces of Artillery, across it, and there waiting the Surrender of the Americans, without firing a Gun, which must have taken place before Night, as they had not any provisions, He placed Gun Boats or floating Batteries in the River directly opposite the Neck of Land aforesaid, & wantonly set fire to Charles Town now wholly deserted by the Inhabitants, and landed about 1800 Men with a large train of Artillery, all well found, with 3 Generals and the best Officers in their Army, early in the Morning at the foot of the Hill on the North East side of the promontory. As soon as the detachment landed, the Fort on Copse [Copp's] Hill in the Town of Boston, which Commanded Breeds Hill at the distance of about a Mile, opened a heavy fire on the Americans. They lay flat on the Ground, without making any Show. Their orders were, not to fire a Gun till the Enemy were within 15 or 20 Yards of their breast work. The Enemy marched up the Hill in a Line, the Grenadiers & light Infantry being in the Center. They appeared very terrible to raw Countrymen; but they observed their orders, and reserved their fire till the Enemy was within a few Yards of their fence. They then suddenly rose, & poured in so terrible a fire of grape & musket shot as to break the Line, and oblige the british to retreat down the Hill. There being no acknowledged Commanding Officer among the Americans every Man did as he pleased; many attended merely to picking out the british Officers, with their Rifles. The Artillery did great Execution. The British rallied about the middle of the Hill, and again advanced, and again met with the same fate. They were rallied a second time, but the British officer Commanding, now seeing his mistake, formed his line into Columns, and advanced once more up the Hill, ashamed & mortified at being thus repulsed by this handful of mere Militia Men. By this time the ammunition of the Americans was nearly expended, especially for the field pieces; a retreat therefore became absolutely necessary. There was no passage to the Main, but over the neck, and thro' the incessant fire of the floating Batteries, with the Enemy pressing them in the rear. Notwithstanding, they pressed on, and made good their retreat & brought off 800 Men out of the 1200, while the British lost 1200 Men & 46 Officers out of 1800 Men. Had the Americans been well supplied with Ammunition, in all probability few of the British would have escaped. Judge Tudor told me, that next morning 15 Grenadiers were found dead in a group, within 15 or 20 feet of the fence.

The View from this Hill is enchanting. You have a full View of Charles Town, Boston, Cambridge Port, Charles River, the Bay, with its Shipping & Islands, and 5 or 6 Bridges.

SEPTEMBER 6 WEDNESDAY. Took another ride, over South Boston Bridge, to Dorchester Neck. The last time I was at this place, was in the face of the Enemy, who was then in possession of Boston. My feelings were now very different, and I enjoyed the beautiful Situation & Scenery around it, with superior delight from the remembrance of its former Circumstances. Instead of viewing the Town & Harbour in possession of a very formidable Enemy and their Victorious Fleet, riding triumphant in our sight, over whom, it was then an extreme doubtful point, whether it was possible for Americans ever to succeed, I now beheld them in far more flourishing Circumstances than ever, with numerous shipping & Coasters crowding the Wharves & enlivening the Harbour, many under full sail on one of the finest days, of our Year, and to crown all, the American Flag waving in our Sight on a formidable Fort commanding the Channel to the Town. Add to this, that Happiness & Comfort seemed to smile all around us, in every Countenance & in every family, and there were none to make them afraid. I could not avoid raising my Heart in gratitude to the great author of all these Mercies, and blessing the God of Heaven, for the unmerited smile of this divine Providence on this happy Land.

The prospects from the point of the Neck are very delightful, and sufficient to tempt every curious Traveller, who comes to Boston, to visit it. This whole promontory or point of Land, wants only, some spirited person who loves his Country, to set the Example, and the whole Tract might be converted into a most luxuriant Spot. The Soil is naturally good, and wants only tillage & manure, to turn the whole into a mere garden. This place is so famous, for having been the means of delivering Boston from its Invaders, that it deserves more Notice than it has received.[149]

[149] In colonial times Dorchester extended into the bay east of Boston Neck as an L-shaped peninsula consisting of Dorchester Neck and Dorchester Heights. During the Siege of Boston the semi-circle of Continental fortifications ran from Dorchester through Roxbury, where General Artemas Ward commanded the right wing, on through Brookline and Cambridge, to Prospect Hill and Winter Hill in Somerville, where General Charles Lee was in command of the left wing. On the night of 4-5 March 1776, while the Ameri-

SEPTEMBER 11 MONDAY. Altho' just able to be carried down to my Carriage, but under great apprehensions of the Winters Coming on, I left this hospitable City and went to Mr Babcocks where I had promised to stay a few days on our Way Home.

Boston is built on a peninsula of irregular form, at the Bottom of Massachusets Bay. The neck of land that joins it to the Continent is at the South End of the Town, leading to Roxbury. Including the Neck, the Town is three miles long, but as it is united with Charles Town & Roxbury, they are together one Continued Street of Buildings of at least five Miles. Boston itself contains about 3000 Houses & 20 000 Inhabitants. There was near as many Houses in it destroyed during the War as were burned in Charles Town. It lies in about 41° 30′ of N. Latitude. There are in it Twenty four places of public worship, most of them well built, with lofty Steeples, some with a Clock, & chiefly with a Bell, as follows—Congregational 9—Episcopal 2—one Calvinistic—a Unitarian calling themselves Episcopal 1[150]—Baptists 4—Methodists 2—Quakers, Roman Catholics,

---

cans kept up a distracting bombardment of Boston, General John Thomas, with two thousand picked men and hundreds of ox-teams, fortified Dorchester Heights, which commanded Boston Harbor and the town. The next day the astonished British made plans for an attack by water, but this was frustrated by a great two-day storm. Boston was now untenable, and on the 17th of March the Commander in Chief of His Majesty's Forces in North America, General Sir William Howe, his troops, and the loyalist inhabitants evacuated the town.

[150] King's Chapel was the first Anglican church in Boston, and dates from 1686. Phillips Brooks wrote in the *Memorial History of Boston* (III, 448) that "It had never been the church of the people, but had largely lived upon the patronage and favor of the English governors." The rector in 1776, Henry Caner (Yale 1724), was evacuated with the rest of the loyalists. In 1783 James Freeman (Harvard 1777) was made pastor and two years later, at his instance, the proprietors adopted and published a prayer book eliminating all references to the Trinity: *A Liturgy Collected principally from the Book of Common Prayer, for the use of the First Episcopal Church in Boston* (Boston, 1785); the church thus became the first Unitarian church in America. Subsequent to the Revolution the edifice was for some time called the Stone Chapel.

Sandemanians, Universalists, & Unitarians, each one. There are also a great number of public Buildings, that beautify the Town —as the State House, the Court House, Concert Hall, Faneuil Hall, Two Theatres, Goal [Gaol], Alms House, Work House, Bridewell, Powder Magazine, The Athenæum,[151] The Museum, The Fish Market, Glass House, and to crown all the Exchange Hotel, a monstrous building containing 212 Rooms, and said to be the most elegant Tavern in the Union.—4 Stories high having 5 Galleries, and is said to have cost $500,000.[152] There are also 7 free Schools having about 900 Scholars. The Congregational Churches prevail thro' out this State. The Ministers have a Meeting in Boston once a Year, on the last Wednesday in May, and a public Sermon on the day following, with a Collection for relieving the necessitous Widows of deceased Ministers. This Convention is a voluntary association, embracing all the Congregational Clergy of the State. They have a Correspondence with the General Assembly of the Presbyterian Church, at Philadelphia, and with the Congregational Ministers in Connecticut, New Hampshire & Vermont. Boston also can

[151] The Boston Athenaeum, a proprietary library, had been founded in 1807, an outgrowth of the Anthology Society, the "Society of Gentlemen" who conducted *The Monthly Anthology and Boston Review*, predecessor of *The North American Review*. In 1809 the Athenaeum had moved from Scollay's Building to the Rufus Greene Amory house north of the King's Chapel Burying Ground; the present literary and scholarly Mecca at 10½ Beacon Street was not opened until 1849.

[152] The Exchange Coffee House was a fabulous establishment for its day and stood on the west side of Congress Street between Water and State. It was a brick Georgian building seven stories high with a rustic basement, six tall marble Ionic pilasters, an entablature with a central pediment, and crowned by a dome which covered and lighted a central court with galleries, from which the rooms opened. The hotel was erected in 1808 and was an immense and dubious speculation floated for a time by the issue of worthless bills by a Rhode Island bank; its destruction in a great fire 3 November 1818 was widely regarded as an act of retribution on the wrong-doers. No lives were lost in the fire, but the next day a small boy was drowned in a great cauldron of beer exposed in the ruins. Josiah Quincy, *Figures of the Past* (Boston, 1926), 34-35; *Memorial History of Boston*, III, 55, 58, 476; Anthology Society of Boston, *Journal* (Boston, 1910), 76.

boast of upwards of thirty benevolent useful & Charitable Societies. They have also five Banks & Six Insurance Offices with 3 private ones.

The Harbour is large & safe, interspersed with upwards of thirty Islands, small & great. On one, is the Castle where the Convicts are kept, about 3 or 4 Miles from the Town. On another, which Commands it, stands a strong fort which also Commands the Channel. On another, stands the Light House about 65 feet high. The Shipping belonging to the Harbour amounts to about 800 Vessels of about 80,000 Tons burthen.

The Town is governed by Nine Select Men & 12 overseers of the poor, all chosen by the Freemen of the Town, annually. On the whole this is one of the most flourishing Towns in the United States, and promises fair to outstrip every other in the Union. Especially when it is considered as only one Sea Port out of Seven, belonging to the State, while New York & Philadelphia are almost the sole Ports of the State, and also takes in the two neighboring States. The Inhabitants seem to have established more of a National Character, than any other Town or State in the union, and they appear to me, likely to become the chief Security of these States.

We continued at Mr Babcocks, with various Company till the 14th when, altho but just able to be lifted into the Carriage, but neither to stand or walk, we set off on our Journey, attended a few Miles by Mr & Mrs Babcock. After taking a most affectionate leave of these kind & dear Friends, we proceeded towards Providence, whither we arrived about 5 oClock, having rode 40 Miles. At Mr Ives's, I got out of the Carriage with difficulty and had to walk a few Yards on my Crutches, which so overcame me, that I had nearly fainted, and it was near an hour, before I came to, so as to attend to the welcome which we received from this kind & agreeable Family.

Mr Thomas P. Ives is a Man of high Character here, one of the first, if not the first Merchant in the Place. His mild, unassuming & amiable Manners justly entitles him to the respect of all with whom he has to do. His integrity is so great, that he is made the general rule, to which the People at large look up to, as an unerring Example. He had the greatest Compliment paid him by a Gentleman in Boston that any Man could expect or desire. We were mentioning Mr. Ives as an exemplary Man. Oh! says he, Mr Ives (as I have heard) is such an Example, that Laws are unnecessary in Providence as his conduct & opinion is considered there as the rule to go by.

SEPTEMBER 16 SATURDAY. We enjoyed ourselves with this agreeable & delightful family, and in visiting every part of the Town till this Morning. When we with reluctance parted with our kind Friends & set our faces homeward. Here we found Miss Binney who had preceeded us a few days to finish her Visit at Providence. She has been highly favoured by a kind Providence, and is surprisingly recruited in point of Health. Her Spirits are fine, and we are again to be gratified with her agreeable Company on the rest of our Journey. It gives us great pleasure, that notwithstanding all our Fears, we hope to be able to return her to her anxious Friends, in tolerable & increasing health. We proceeded on our Journey by the same road that we came, till we passed Lebanon & came near to Columbia. We could not help indulging some melancholy thoughts, and sincerely condole with the bereaved & distressed Family of Govr. Trumbul, as we passed thro' Lebanon. Since our late Visit, the Govr. had been seized violently with his disorder again, which had closed his useful Life about 2 or 3 weeks after we left him.[153] Such was his life, as to afford the strongest consolations in his death, and we doubt not he is gone to receive the blessed reward of a useful & well spent life. Blessed are the dead who die in the Lord!

Columbia is a small Village with a large Church. The roads continued good. We dined at Eatons Tavern, and then passed

[153] Governor Trumbull died at his home in Lebanon 7 August 1809.

thro' Jewets City, being on the Turnpike, which unfortunately
for us, Eaton advised us to keep. This was 7 Miles from Norwich and we soon entered the roughest & most mountainous
Country we had yet met with. The Mountain was more than a
Mile higher than the road we had left, very steep & broken and
continued quite to Norwich. It is said to be a turnpike road, and
you are made to pay an extravagant toll, but it is but the bare
name of a Turnpike, and the old road is far preferable. It took
us as long to travel these 7 Miles, as it did 10 Miles on the other
road. Being overtaken by the night, and it becoming very dark
on the Top of the Mountain, we were obliged to go very slow,
and did not reach Norwich till 8 oClock. We had rode 45 Miles,
and were greatly overcome with fatigue. This was in a great
measure alleviated, by the extreme kindness of our Friends.[154]
They received us as parts of their family, and made us most
heartily welcome. Here we remained till Monday Morning.

SEPTEMBER 18 MONDAY. We again took to our Carriage and
arrived at Hartford in the Evening, after a very pleasant ride,
the Weather being very fine.

SEPTEMBER 19 TUESDAY. This Morning we took (by advice)
a new road, as passing thro' a very thick settled Country—this is
called the Farmington turnpike, and is 39 Miles to New Haven.
At 4 Miles we passed thro' West Hartford, along a very pleasant & good Road. It has a large Church, School House, a large
Tavern and several good Houses. At 5 Miles farther on an excellent Road, we opened a most beautiful Vale, surrounded by a
grand amphitheatre of high Hills, seemingly well cultivated
and thickly set with Houses. A most delightful prospect continued till we came to Farmington at one Mile farther. This is
a handsome Village with a well built large Church, a School
House, and about 100 Houses, 50 of which are really fine
Houses and 4 of them superbly elegant. I was surprised to ob-
serve almost every sign in the Town, and there was no less than

---

[154] Probably Mrs. Austin and her mother.

a dozen, all of the name of *Cowles*. A most delightful Vale of
about 4 Miles wide and an elegant turnpike road, gave us great
pleasure and many agreeable observations, till we arrived at
Southington at 9 Miles from Farmington. Here we dined at
the Widow Lewis's, a good House. This is a large Village with
a long string of Houses and three Churches—an Episcopal,
Presbyterian & Baptist—the 2d had a very handsome Steeple &
Spire. At 6 Miles, road good & fine Country, we passed thro'
Cheshire. Here are two large Churches, a large Brick Accademy
& School House. About 40 or 50 Houses. The prospects continue very fine. The Town is situated on a lofty Hill, and the
Intervale Lands all around, well cultivated, beautiful & thickly
settled. For several Miles further, the Houses on each side of
the road, are within 4 or 500 yards of each other, like a continued Street. At 8 Miles from New Haven came to Hampden,
where there are 2 Churches a Presbyterian & Episcopal and
a large School House.

The Mountain on the left, all the way from a little below
Cheshire, terminates near this place, with a high Bluff called
Mount Carmel, and affords a very romantic Scenery. We were
informed that this Bluff is between 4 & 500 feet in heigth and
is well calculated to gratify the Curious Travellers.

We arrived at New Haven, and found Judge Chauncey quite
full with a number of Friends, who had come in from the Country to see a review, to take place the next day. We went again
to Butlers Tavern & were again refused Entertainment on Account of the review. He sent us to another House & they to a
third, till the darkness coming on, we began to think we should
not get any Quarters at any rate. At length we were recom-
mended to an Inferior Tavern, in the Skirt of the Town. Here
we were again refused, but on Mr. Buck the Tavern keeper
hearing that there was a sick Gent'n in the Carriage, he took us
in. We found ourselves in very good Quarters & entertained
with as much kindness & attention, as if we had been in the

first Tavern in the State. We had good Beds & every thing clean
& neat. Our Landlady made an Excuse for her Husband having
refused us, on Account of an Agreement between them never
again to take in Ladies from the Southard. The reason she assigned was, the extreme hateur & uncivil behaviour of some
Ladies from New York, as to determine them in this measure.
Travellers should remember, that Tavern keepers are entitled
to decent behaviour, as well as other People—and that by this
ungenteel Conduct they injure more prudent Travellers.

SEPTEMBER 20 WEDNESDAY. We left New Haven at 1/2 past
10 oClock, altho' we had intended to have staid the Day at least,
but being informed that the review was to be of 5000 Men &
would last two days, we thought it prudent to decamp. Within
4 Miles from Stratford, we went thro' Milford, which I neglected to mention in going out. Here are 3 Churches 2 Congregational & 1 Episcopal, and a long string of Houses that
make a good Appearance. We dined at Lovejoys. I asked after
Dr. Johnston, who I supposed had been dead some time, but
was astonished to be told by our Landlady, that she had seen
him, the day before, galloping his Horse thro the Town. I immediately sent my Servant to let him know that I was at the
Tavern, but unable to call on him. He soon came in, as lively as
a Man of fifty. We were rejoyced to see each other in the flesh
again, and could not help remarking on the uncertainty of human things. On my way thro', I had left him apparently in the
Arms of death, in the last stage of the Gout. And now he was
visiting me in the same disorder.

Dr. Johnston informed us, that after our departure, he grew
worse & worse, till the Gout seized him wholly in the Breast. He
prepared himself for death, and his Friends surrounded his Bed,
expecting every Moment would be the last. To relieve the ex-
tremity of Pain, they gave him a considerable draught of Brandy.
This brought him to, which he thought merely a temporary relief, but the paroxysm did not return, and he revived, and is

now as lively & active as could be expected at the Age of Eighty two—Except that his hands are left in a very contracted State, by the late severity of the Disorder.[155]

After Dinner we proceeded to Norwalk, and arrived at Motts a quarter before Six oClock. Here we enjoyed a very comfortable Night.

SEPTEMBER 21 THURSDAY. We went on the former road, and arrived at New Rochelle early in the Evening, to the great Joy of our Friends, who had been fearing, that I was laid up on the road. Here we staid, enjoying the Society of our Friends, till the 25th when we again parted with those we love, and after stopping at Mr. Wm Ogdens a half an Hour & finding him & Mother very ill, we passed the North River from New York to Hoboken in 20 Minutes, thus making up, in some Measure, for our untoward passage in our outward Journey. We arrived at New Ark just before Tea, and were received with open Arms by our relatives. Here we again enjoyed ourselves, finding that we had got again into New Jersey and so near our wished for Home,—till the

29 When after a pleasant ride, on a fine day & excellent Roads, we arrived at Princeton. Soon after I got in, I was seized with a severe paroxysm of the Gout in my Breast, having taken a little Cold in crossing the North River. I suffered exceedingly 2 Nights & 2 Days, but then got relief and on

OCTOBER 2 Set off again and arrived at our long desired Habitation by the middle of the Afternoon, having been absent just 100 Days. We found our Family and Friends assembled to receive us, which they did with a most hearty welcome and in the most joyful manner.

It is not among the least of the Mercies, that we have to be thankful for during our Absence, that our domestics have all behaved very well. Our Neighbours and Friends speak in the

---

[155] William Samuel Johnson lived on for another ten years, and died at Stratford 14 November 1819 in his ninety-third year.

best manner of their orderly Conduct & industrious attention to the Charge left with them.

Our Friends indeed have paid great attention also, to them & all our little affairs about our House, Garden & Fields—for which we feel great thankfulness, and are much obliged by them, and shall always be ready to return the favour whenever in our power, with Interest.

Miss Binney & Mrs. Bradford have borne the fatigue of this Journey out & in, with surprising firmness. Miss Binney is an Instance of Gods goodness & Mercy, as when we set out, I had but little hope of taking her farther than New Rochelle. She now promises fair to regain her health, if she is prudent thro' the Winter.

Thus hath a gracious God preserved us all at home & abroad, and made us the living Monuments of his sparing goodness.

Return unto thy rest, o my Soul, for the Lord hath dealt bountifully with thee.

I was brought low and he helped me, what shall I render unto the Lord, for his benefits towards me?

Oh! that Men would praise the Lord for his goodness, and for his wonderful works to the Children of Men.

Bless the Lord, O my Soul, and all that is within me, bless his holy Name.

Bless the Lord, O my Soul, and forget not all his benefits.

Bless the Lord all his Works, in all places of his dominion. Bless the Lord, O my Soul.

FINIS.

INDEX

Abbot, Benjamin, 64

Abbot, Samuel, 69, 70

Adams, John, vii, viii, 35n, 42-46, 56n, 58, 61; Mrs. (Abigail Smith), 3n, 44, 46

Adams, John Quincy, 42n, 46n, 47

Adams, Samuel, 75n

Albany, N.Y., 30n

Albemarle, Duke of, 71

America, warship, 60

American Bible Society, x, xv

Ames, Fisher, 31-32, 45

Ames, Nathaniel, 31n

Amherst College, 65n

Amory, Rufus Greene, 80n

Andover, Conn., 20

Andover, Mass., 64-71

Andover Theological Seminary, 1, 65-70

Anglicans and Episcopalians, 7n, 9, 43-44n, 79n

Anthology Society, Boston, 35n, 45n, 80n

Astley, Thomas, 33n

Auburn Theological Seminary, 1n

Austin, David, 22-23; Mrs. (Lydia Lathrop), 22, 23, 26, 83

Babcock, Adam, 34, 35, 38, 40, 43, 44, 50, 72, 73, 79, 81; Mrs. (Martha Hubbard), 33, 35n, 40, 43, 81

Babcock, Eliza (Mrs. Nathaniel Ingersoll), 44n

Babcock, Francis, 36; Mrs. (Alice Wyer), 36n

Babcock, Joshua, 35n

Babcock, Louisa, 36

Babcock, Luke, 35n

Babcock, Martha Hubbard (Mrs. George Higginson; Mrs. James Perkins Higginson), 36, 38-40, 45

Babcock, Mary Greene (Mrs. John Gore), 40, 72

Bache, Theophylact, 3n

Backus, Eunice (Mrs. Jonathan Trumbull Jr.), 21

Baldwin, Ashbel, 7

Baltimore, 50n

Bancroft, George, 64n

Barnes, David Leonard, 29, 30n, 38

Barrell, Colborn, Mrs. (Elizabeth Langdon), 62, 63

Bartlet, William, 69

Batchelder, Samuel Francis, 53n

Bayard, Samuel, vii, 45; Mrs. (Martha Pintard), 45n

Beacon Hill, Boston, 34-35n, 40n, 41

Benedict, W. H., 3n

Bentley, William, 28n, 69n

Berkeley Hall, Yale, 17n

Berlin, Conn., 19

Bernard, Sir Francis, 33n

Berwick, Maine, 63

Beverly, Mass., 55

Bill, Elizabeth (Mrs. Daniel Lathrop Coit), 22n, 23, 25

Bill, Hannah (Mrs. Thomas Lathrop), 22n, 23

Binney, Barnabas, 32n

Binney, Horace, 32n

Binney, Mary, viii, xi, 1, 3, 10, 25, 26, 32, 43, 47, 49, 82, 87

Binney, Mary (Woodrow), (Mrs. Marshall Spring), 32n

Binney, Susan (Mrs. J. B. Wallace), 32n, 45n

Blaxton, William, 34n

Bodleian Library, 48n

Bolton, Conn., 20

Bond, Henry, 32n

Boston, 4, 18n, 30n, 33-53, 55, 64, 65n, 66, 69n, 71-73, 76-81

Boston, Siege of, 78n

Boston & Providence Railroad, 13n

Boston Athenaeum, 80

Boston Bay and Harbor, 76, 77, 79n, 81

Boston Light, 81

Boston Neck, 78n, 79

"Boston religion," 51n

Boudinot, Annis (Mrs. Richard Stockton), 1n

Boudinot, Elias, Mrs. (Hannah Stockton), vii, ix, 1n

Boudinot, Elisha, xi, 1n, 42, 44, 45n; Mrs. (Rachel Bradford), 45n

Boudinot, Susan Vergereau (Mrs. William Bradford Jr.), viii, x-xi, 1, 8, 10, 34, 45, 70, 87

Bowdoin, James, 49n

Bowdoin College, 67n

Bowen, Jabez, 29, 30n

Boyd, George Adams, viii, xiii

Bozrah, Conn., 23n

Bradford, Mass., 65